A Rivalry of Genius

SUNY Series in Judaica: Hermeneutics, Mysticism, and Religion

Michael Fishbane, Robert Goldenberg, and Elliot Wolfson, Editors

A Rivalry of Genius

Jewish and Christian Biblical Interpretation in Late Antiquity

Marc Hirshman

Translated by Batya Stein

STATE UNIVERSITY OF NEW YORK PRESS

Published by
State University of New York Press, Albany

For information, address State University of New York Press,
State University Plaza, Albany, N.Y. 12246

Production by M. R. Mulholland
Marketing by Bernadette La Manna

Library of Congress Cataloging-in-Publication Data

Hirshman, Marc G.
    [Miķra u-midrasho. English]
    A rivalry of genius : Jewish and Christian biblical interpretation
in late antiquity / Marc Hirshman.
        p.   cm. — (SUNY series in Judaica)
    Includes bibliographical references (p.   ) and index.
    ISBN 0-7914-2727-7. — ISBN 0-7914-2728-5 (pbk.)
    1. Midrash—Comparative studies.   2. Bible. O.T.—Criticism,
interpretation, etc., Jewish.   3. Bible. O.T.—Criticism,
interpretation, etc.—History—Early church, ca. 30-600.   4. Fathers
of the church.   I. Title.   II. Series.
    BM514.H5713   1996
    221.6'09—dc20   95-5271
                                                                  CIP

10 9 8 7 6 5 4 3 2 1

Contents

Preface

This study began in 1985 as an attempt to determine whether Procopius of Gaza was influenced by the format of Jewish Midrash when he inaugurated his *catena* literature.

While analyzing all of Procopius' sources, I was struck by the diverse formats of literary creativity within which the Church housed its biblical exegeses. Those ranged from homilies to school lectures to letters, biographies, and histories. Indeed, the full range of Greco-Roman literary genres was enlisted to serve as a vehicle for Christian biblical exegeses.

In stark contrast, rabbinic exegesis had confined itself strictly to the literary format called *Midrash*. This seemed to me, then as now, a conscious effort on the part of the rabbis of the land of Israel of the first five centuries to isolate themselves literarily from the regnant culture. Though Greek and Roman culture influenced the rabbis, as Saul Lieberman has amply shown, they restricted their oral (and written) aggadic creativity to the one basic format of Midrash collections and scriptural interpretations. I will not at this point address their other major creative formats—the Mishnah and the Talmud.

This monograph was an attempt to present the literary contrasts between the Church and the Jewish sages to the modern Hebrew readers. The editor of the Hebrew series, Meir Ayali, invited me to broaden the scope, so that the book would serve as a survey of some of the literary relationships between rabbinic Midrash and patristic exegesis in late antiquity

My focus was on the Church Fathers who were either born or lived in Palestine of the third to the fifth centuries—Justin Martyr, Origen, and Jerome. While highlighting the study of genres, I have tried to canvas other issues, such as polemics and borrowing between the two religious traditions. It remains my conviction that the comparative study of exegetical creativity in Judaism and Christianity of antiquity immeasurably enriches our understanding of these religions and of the Bible itself.

This book has been translated with exceptional care by Batya Stein. I am thankful to her and to the editors and management of SUNY Press for their care and attention to the manuscript. I have not added to the original Hebrew work or made any major changes, except for Chapter 1, which was reworked from a Hebrew essay published in *Mahanayim* 7 (1994). I have though on occasion departed from the standard translations of the rabbinic works when necessary. Chapter 2 offers an overview of rabbinic and patristic literary creativity, concentrating on their respective claims to exclusivity and uniqueness. In Chapter 3 I discuss the midrashic styles of these two traditions, drawing a distinction between two very different aspects: the techniques used to decode the text, and the rhetorical devices used to present their results. A Christian homilist, preaching in Greek within the conventions of Greek rhetoric, differs from a Jewish homilist, preaching in Aramaic (or in Hebrew?) before a Jewish audience. The discussion will point out the contrast between the broad variety of Christian homiletical works, as opposed to the largely uniform style of the Jewish collections that include homilies and commentaries. I also portray in this chapter the leading Christian spokesmen, leaving the description of their times and languages for a later stage.

In Chapters 4 to 6 I concentrate on Justin Martyr's important work, *Dialogue with Trypho*, which highlights the intensity of the exegetic dispute involving Christians and Jews, as it appeared to a second-century Christian. Justin's homilies are contrasted with rabbinic ones found in the Mekhilta and Genesis Rabbah, to stress the differences in their approaches to common exegetic problems in Scripture.

Chapters 7 and 8 are devoted to Origen, one of the spiritual giants of the Church who lived and wrote in Caesarea in the third and fourth decades of the third century. Origen was greatly interested in Jewish exegesis and devoted himself to the understanding of Scripture, including the Hebrew original. Judging by his homilies and commentaries, he must have posed a great challenge to the Jewish community of his time.

In his commentary on Ecclesiastes, Jerome cites many Jewish teachings that he learned from his Hebrew tutor. In Chapter 9 I compare Jerome's exegesis and the rabbinic exegesis of Ecclesiastes.

Chapter 10 sums up the story of the biblical encounter depicted in this book. Four other Church figures are also reviewed briefly, emphasizing the differences in the genres of their works. We also glance at the schools that developed in the Syrian Church and deal with two other Christian authors who lived in Palestine. Two appendices deal with methodological problems surrounding the study of the religious controversy and the exegesis of Scripture.

I was encouraged by my colleagues in the study of Rabbinics and Patristics who felt that this work should be made available in English. I thank them, and especially Caroline Hammond Bammel, Jeremy Cohen, Shaye Cohen, N. R. M. de Lange, Joshua Levinson, David Satran, Jane Shapiro, and Hayim Goldgraber for their help and advice. Paula Fredriksen deserves a special thanks for her important comments and careful reading. My mentors, Haim Zalman Dimitrovsky and David Weiss-Halivni, continue to grace me with their advice and erudition. The memory of my two revered teachers, Saul Lieberman and Moshe Zucker constantly reminds me of what true scholarship can achieve.

In the preface to the Hebrew version, I thanked my family and friends in Israel, England, and the United States for their support and help. Over the past few years I have made frequent trips to the United States and have been warmly received and supported by the Jewish Theological Seminary and its Chancellor Ismar Schorsch and by the East Brunswick Jewish Center and its rabbi, my friend Chaim Rogoff, and his family. I am grateful to SUNY Press and the Jack and Celia Rogoff Memorial Fund for contributing to this translation.

I dedicate this volume with love and admiration to my father Morry Hirshman and his wife Doris, and to my mother Florence Goldman Hirshman, of blessed memory.

1

Biblical Interpretation in Its Late Antique Context

During the rabbinic period, and as late as the Middle Ages, Jews and Christians fought a relentless battle over the question, What is the true and correct interpretation of Scripture?

To the casual onlooker, the controversy between Jews and Christians in the first centuries C.E. appeared quite preposterous. The Jews had not yet recovered from the harsh defeats they had suffered in the wars of 70 and 132 C.E., and they were forced to contend with the painful humiliation of a pagan temple on the site of their Temple in Jerusalem. The Christians were perceived by the Romans as subversive, nothing less than the enemies of humanity. They were often persecuted and put to death merely because they confessed to being Christians. The pretension of both Christians and Jews to be God's chosen evoked derision in the pagan listener,[1] for whom the supremacy of the empire irrefutably proved that disputes between Jews and Christians were a ludicrous farce played out by self-deluding losers.

Celsus, the second-century pagan philosopher, claimed that one could compare

> the race of Jews and Christians to a cluster of bats or ants coming out of a nest, or frogs holding council round a marsh, or worms assembling in some filthy corner, disagreeing with one another about which of them are the worse sinners. They say: "God shows and proclaims everything to us beforehand, and He has even deserted the whole world and the motion of the heavens, and disregarded the vast earth to give attention to us alone.... There is God first, and we are next after Him in rank since He has made us entirely like God, and all things have been put under us, earth, water, air, and stars; and all

things exist for our benefit, and have been appointed to serve us.... All these assertions would be more tolerable coming from worms and frogs than from Jews and Christians disagreeing with one another.[2]

These unflattering remarks are faithfully echoed in the words of Christianity's greatest foe, the Roman emperor Julian, who wrote an entire treatise attacking Christianity entitled *Against the Galilaeans.* Julian, whom Christians call "The Apostate," writes in the year 362:[3]

Therefore it is fair to ask of Paul why God, if He was not the God of the Jews only but also of the Gentiles, sent the blessed gift of prophecy to the Jews in abundance and gave them Moses and the oil of anointing, and the prophets and the law and the incredible and monstrous elements in their myths?... but unto us no prophet, no oil of anointing, no teacher, no herald to announce his love for man which should one day, though late, reach even unto us also. Nay, he even looked on for myriads, or if you prefer, for thousands of years, while men in extreme ignorance served idols, as you call them, from where the sun rises to where he sets, yes and from North to South, save only that little tribe which less than two thousand years before had settled in one part of Palestine...

These pagan attacks against Christians and Jews have survived only because Church dignitaries saw fit to disprove them in works specifically written for this purpose. Our knowledge of Julian's and Celsus' arguments is thus secondhand, coming from Christian works devoted to the refutation of pagan claims.

We must note that the Jewish and Christian battle for supremacy, for the right to be called *Israel,* for the ownership of Scripture and its true interpretation, was not waged in isolation. Pagans attacked both religions for their pretense that only one of them was privy to the authentic revelation. Pagan thinkers were appalled by the insolence of both Jewish and Christian claims to ascendancy and closeness to God, when their real-life situation, at least in political terms, was at its lowest ebb.

G. Stroumsa has recently noted that the end of the second century, when Celsus' work was published, is also the time when decisions were being made about the canon of the New Testament on the one hand, and the Oral Law on the other.[4] According to this thesis, both religions attempted to cast their doctrines in clear, defined terms. If we follow this line of thought, we might say that the need of both religions to define themselves, vis-à-vis the competitor as well as vis-à-vis the external pagan threat, gave special impetus to the creation of written and oral collections of their sacred teachings.

Another element affecting the development of both religions in this period was Gnosis (Greek for knowledge). Gnostics claimed that the God of Scripture was a bad God—jealous, vengeful, and begrudging. He was the demiurge, the god that created the universe and chose Israel, but not the true, good God. The good God, the true Master of the Universe, was unknown except through revelation, and could be approached only by the gnostic, who possesses the necessary knowledge. Up to fifty years ago, our knowledge of Gnosticism relied on the writings of the Church Fathers who had attempted to refute it. A few years before the discovery of the Dead Sea Scrolls, however, gnostic texts were discovered in Egypt written on 1500-year-old papyri. This discovery at Nag Hammadi has greatly enriched our knowledge of gnostic exegesis. This selection from the gnostic interpretation of the story of paradise appears in a text entitled *The Hypostasis of the Archons* (that is, the nature or source of rulers[5]) apparently written in the third century: "Their chief [the archons'] is blind; [because of his] Power and his ignorance [and his] arrogance he said with his [Power] 'It is I who am God; there is none [apart from me].' When he said this he sinned against [the Entirety]. And this speech got to Incorruptibility; then there was a voice that came forth from Incorruptibility, saying, 'You are mistaken, Samael'—which is 'god of the blind.'"[6] We are then told that Samael descends into the chaos and the abyss, his mother, while the "incorruptible" looks down and his image is reflected in the water. The forces of darkness fall in love with this image and decide—"let us make man." But the archons, who rule over the forces of darkness, could neither move nor raise this creature, until the Master of the Universe, in his great mercy according to one version, took pity and breathed into it the breath of life. The archons then placed man in paradise and, as we know, commanded him not to eat from the tree of knowledge (although the father, the Master of the Universe, did want him to know good and evil). After the sin, the chief archon came and asked man, "Man, where art thou?" because he did not understand what had happened.

Let us summarize the principles of the Gnostic approach as they emerge from this exegesis of the story of the Creation and paradise, even if many colorful details have been deleted. We should not allow the odd and exotic to dull the power of the gnostic exegesis of this story, as well as the dangers it posed in its day. The serpent, according to Gnosis, speaks the truth; god the creator is jealous of his creatures and does not wish them to attain knowledge, the more so because his own knowledge is limited. Irrefutable proof of god's limitations is the very question, "Man, where art thou?" Man's expulsion from paradise on the suspicion that "the man is become like one of us, knowing good and evil: and now, what if he put forth his hand, and take also of the tree of life, and eating, live for ever" (Genesis 3:22) shows this is an evil god, jealous of his creatures. The good God, the Master of the Universe, is in hiding and can be reached only through wisdom and knowledge.

The rabbis sensed the problematic entailed by the phrase *Where art thou?* [*ayeka?*], and explain its derivation from the root *ekh* (how). According to this homily, the Holy One, blessed be He, turns to man and asks him "How [*ekh*] has this happened to you? Yesterday thou wast ruled by my will, and now by the will of the serpent..." (*Genesis Rabbah* 19,9).[7] Further on, this midrash expounds *ekh* as *ekha*, which is the word that opens the Book of Lamentations, and creates a remarkable parallel between Adam and the people of Israel: "just as I led Adam into the garden of Eden and commanded him, and he transgressed My commandments, whereupon I punished him by dismissal and expulsion, and bewailed him with *ekhah*...so also did I bring his descendants into Eretz Yisrael and commanded them, and they transgressed My commandment, and I punished them by sending them away and expelling them, and I bewailed them with *ekhah*!" (*Genesis Rabbah*, 19,9). This homily, which plays with the vocalization of the word *ayeka*, exposes a theological infrastructure crucial to the understanding of Scripture, whereby Adam's action is a lesson to his children, the people of Israel. The story of paradise is an archetype that anticipates the story of Israel in their land, and their expulsion from it. This is a fine example of free, even fanciful exegesis, which might, in a broad stroke, reveal hidden but "intended" meanings in the Bible.

Chrysostom, a fourth century Church Father known for his antipathy toward and rivalry with the Jews of Antioch, invests enormous efforts in an attempt to present the story of paradise as actually indicating God's love for humanity (*philanthropia*): God enters into a dialogue with humankind, "Adam, where art thou" (according to the Septuagint version which adds the word *Adam*), and attempts to cure the disease immediately, before it spreads. Incidentally, it is of note that Chrysostom uses the same homily we quoted from *Genesis Rabbah*—"How has this happened to you?"—which I believe he learned from Jewish sources.[8]

On the one hand, rabbinic midrashim and Christian exegeses both fought the pagan enemy, the outsider, who denied the legitimacy of their own interpretations and saw them merely as myths and fabrications. On the other hand, both religions were threatened by the well-developed mythological structure of Gnosis, which interpreted Scripture and even some of the Christian works as speaking of an evil demiurge—the God of Israel.

Jewish or Christian sages expounding Scripture in the first few centuries C.E. thus had to contend with three external factors challenging their exegetic approach, as well as their conclusions and theology. Questions may be raised about the literary reality of the period. Were the homilists of the time aware of their ideological rivals? Perhaps the rabbinic and Christian texts that have reached us were meant for their communities alone? Maybe they ignored disputing views and expounded Scripture without any polemical concerns?

Before attempting to answer I would like to clarify that I am only interested in the literary creations of the two religions. Does this literature attest to any awareness of exegetic rivals outside Judaism or Christianity? Indeed, awareness of other exegetic trends and of the challenges posed by their rivals is pervasive in both rabbinic and Christian literature. Let me offer some examples.

No event is more important to the rabbis than the revelation at Sinai. Scripture describes the occasion when the Holy One, blessed be He, was revealed before the whole people and gave them the Torah. Scripture does not explicitly state why, of all nations on earth, the Torah was given to this particular people on this unique occasion. The rabbis were troubled by this problem and offered a variety of answers, which cannot be exhausted within the scope of the present work. I will cite two bearing directly on our concerns—the rabbis' consideration for their rivals and for their arguments.

We read in the *Mekhilta de Rabbi Ishmael*, a Palestinian commentary on Exodus edited in the middle of the third century: "Why was the Torah not given in the land of Israel? In order that the nations of the world should have no excuse for saying: Because it was given in Israel's land, therefore we have not accepted it.... To three things the Torah is likened: To the desert, to fire and to water. This is to tell you that just as these three things are free to all who come into the world, so also are the words of the Torah free to all who come into the world."[9] A bit earlier we find the famous legend claiming that the Holy One, blessed be He, offered the Torah to all the nations and they refused; only Israel took on the yoke of the commandments. In the words of the *Mekhilta*, "And the nations of the world were asked to accept the Torah in order that they should have no excuse for saying, Had we been asked we would have accepted it..."[10] These texts show that the rabbis not only took into account the claims of their rivals in antiquity, but also quoted them in their name—"the nations of the world." This is one instance of a trend that was quite prominent in the rabbinic exegesis of the Sinai theophany. The rabbis dealt with the question that the nations' writers insisted on asking: Why does the Creator bestow all His grace on one nation while neglecting all the others? Not only do the homilies in the *Mekhilta* contend with this question, but the Midrash identifies the rival by name "in order that the nations of the world should have no excuse."

This is also true of the gnostic and Christian threats. In some cases, explicit mention is made of Jesus ("son of Pantera") and his disciples.[11] The most famous example is found in the *Tosefta*, that cardinal tannaitic work which parallels and complements the *Mishnah* and was codified a generation after it (in the middle of the third century C.E.): "R. Eliezer was arrested for heresy and brought to judgment. The *hegemon* said to him, 'Should an old man like you get involved in such things?' Said he [R. Eliezer]: 'I rely on the Judge...' He [the *hegemon*] said to him: 'Since you have deemed me reliable...dismissed—you are pardoned' (*Tosefta Hullin* 2:24)."

Lieberman has already explained this story in light of the procedures of Roman law at the time.[12] R. Eliezer was suspected of "heresy" here to be interpreted as association with Christianity, an illicit religion according to the Romans.[13] A double entendre saves R. Eliezer, but he is tormented by the notion that suspicions could have been cast on him at all. R. Akiva, his disciple, attempts to comfort him: "He said to him [R. Akiva to R. Eliezer], 'Perhaps one of the heretics told you some words of heresy which pleased you?' He [R. Eliezer] said 'By Heaven! You remind me. Once I was strolling in the street of Sepphoris and met Jacob of Kefar Sikhnin, and he told me a teaching of heresy in the name of Jesus son of Panteri,[14] and it pleased me, and so I was arrested on account of heresy.'"

A later midrash, as well as the Babylonian Talmud, claim to preserve the very same homily Jacob told R. Eliezer in the name of Jesus. In the *Tosefta* rendition, R. Eliezer admits that he had listened to and derived pleasure from the words of "Torah" delivered in Jesus' name. The purpose of this story seems clear. It is to deter observant Jews from conducting a dialogue with Christians, especially concerning Scripture. Who, after all, is greater than R. Eliezer b. Hyrcanus, and even he was arrested by the Roman authorities on suspicion of heresy, because he lent his ear to one of their exegeses? Stories of this kind were probably used to warn Jews against developing contacts or engaging in confrontations with Christians regarding Scripture.[15]

This story from the *Tosefta* is the exception however. Much more often, rabbinic literature deals with the threat posed by heretics [*minim*]. Although the identification of these heretics is not always certain, in many instances they unquestionably stand for Christians or gnostics.[16] In the same discussion, when considering the giving of the Torah and the practice of reading the Ten Commandments, the rabbis contend with the heretics' claims: "R. Nathan says, From here is a refutation to the heretics who say:

There are two powers. For when the Holy One, blessed be he, stood up and said: 'I am the Lord your God,' was there anyone who stood up to protest against Him? If you should say that it was done in secret, it has already been said: 'I have not spoken in secret...'" (*Mekhilta de-Rabbi Ishmael*, ibid.).[17] It is the gnostics who speak of two powers. The gnostic myth on paradise quoted previously now takes on new brilliance. As soon as the archon Samael claims exclusivity and says "It is I who am God," a voice immediately answers back from Heaven: "You are mistaken, Samael." The author of the gnostic text seems to have heard R. Nathan's question—"Was there anyone who stood up to protest against Him?"—and responded that the hidden incorruptible God did stand up to the God of Israel and showed He was mistaken.

The rabbis were not only concerned with answering their rivals' questions regarding theoretical issues and scriptural exegeses, but also present themselves as enacting legal (halakhic) rulings in response to the threat posed by the heretics. Urbach discusses the tradition of the Babylonian and Palestinian Talmuds, which reports that the daily reading of the Ten Commandments was abolished due to "the imputation of the heretics, that they should not say that only these [the Ten Commandments] were given to Moses at Sinai."[18] In other words, Palestinian *amoraim* claimed that the practice of reading the Ten Commandments (Deuteronomy 5) along with *Keri'at Shema* (Deuteronomy 6), which is already mentioned in the *Mishnah* (Tamid 5:1), was abolished because of the heretics. For our purposes, whether this is indeed the true reason for canceling this practice is irrelevant. Suffice it to say that, in the consciousness of Palestinian as well as Babylonian *amoraim*, contending with heretics demanded not only theoretical answers but also practical measures.

I have so far tried to show that rabbinic literature mentions its ideological rivals in antiquity and openly contends with their claims. The "later" midrash mentioned earlier is *Ecclesiastes Rabbah* (redacted c. seventh century), where we read explicitly of a *tanna* with whom "the heretics used to have dealings. They would ask him questions and he would answer, ask him and he would answer" (1:8), very much in the model of medieval disputations. And even the Church Fathers, for their part, attest to discussions with the Jews. Origen, who lived in Caesarea in the thirties and forties of the third century, discusses the meaning of the word *Pesah*: "Should anyone of us, when meeting the Jews, hastily say that the Passover is thus named after the suffering of the Savior, they laugh at him as one who does not understand the meaning of the word, when they believe that, as Jews, they interpret the name correctly."[19] Origen tried to ensure that Christians would not be ridiculed in dialogue with Jews because they were using unreliable translations of the Hebrew text of Scripture. In this instance, Christians identified the sacrifice of Passover with the "sacrifice" of Jesus, who was crucified on or just before Passover according to the different traditions. Christians saw incontrovertible evidence for this in the fact that the Hebrew word pesah itself hints to their Saviour's pain, since its Greek homophone means suffering (*Paschein*). Origen pointed out that, in Hebrew, *pesah* means "passage" and relied on the literal meaning of the Hebrew word in his own Greek homily. On the other hand, Origen also directs his barbs against those Jews who think that they have interpreted this verse correctly. In his eyes, the Jews understand only the bare words but completely miss their import. The Christians understand the message but only through their reading of the Septuagint.

Evidence indicates that Church Fathers were sensitive to the educational needs of Christians who were involved in disputes with Jews. The *Tosefta*, edited close to Origen's times, makes patently clear that Jews and Christians met around Scripture.

Christians had to defend themselves against gnostics and pagans, while at the same time contending with Jewish views. The titles of many Christian writings dating from the end of the second through the fifth centuries show that they were directed against gnostics. At the end of the second century, Irenaeus of Lyon writes an extensive treatise against heretics, and his contemporary, Tertullian of Carthage, writes a five-volume work against Marcion, a leading figure in Gnosis. The great Christian directory of heresies in late antiquity was composed by the fourth century bishop Epiphanius, born in Eleutheropolis, Palestine. Epiphanius brings together in one volume an account of all heretical sects, classifies them, and confutes their views. His work, entitled *Panarion* [The Medicine Chest], is meant to serve as a remedy against heretical fallacies. Epiphanius counts eighty heresies—as the number of Solomon's mistresses in the Song of Songs.[20]

The literary phenomenon I have just described brings to the fore a clear distinction between Christianity and Judaism. Both religions claimed to engage in the true interpretation of Scripture and devoted enormous efforts to developing creative exegeses. The Church, however, did not confine itself to scriptural commentaries and conducted a full-scale war, in the shape of whole tracts dedicated to refuting gnostic exegeses and blackening the gnostics' reputation. Christians wrote in Greek and Latin and using genres from their native Greco-Roman culture to support their claims. These genres included dialogues, such as the *Dialogue with Trypho*; attacks against rivals, such as the works by Tertullian and Irenaeus mentioned previously, and apologia, monographs defending their religion. This difference between the literature of Judaism and that of Christianity seems to be one of the central reasons for Christianity's acceptance among Roman citizens, which eventually led to it becoming the official religion of the Roman empire at the end of the fourth century. The way to this ascendancy was paved by many Christian writings addressed to an educated public, offering ways to understand Scripture together with systematic arguments, elegantly styled, endorsing their own views and rejecting rival doctrines. Some historians have claimed, and I support this view, that Jews during this period also succeeded in attracting many proselytes from among the surrounding nations.[21] Nevertheless, we have no evidence of any rabbinic attempt to compose special texts, such as the monographs of Christian authors, attacking their rivals or sustaining their own claims. The rabbis remained within the literary framework they had fixed for themselves and formulated their arguments as well as their principles of faith mainly as scriptural exegeses.

The third type of Christian writings mentioned, the apologia, gave their name to the second-century Church Fathers, known as the *apologists*. During the second and the beginning of the third centuries, Christianity was a persecuted, illegal religion in the Roman empire. Justin Martyr, born in Shechem, Palestine, in the second century, was sentenced to death in Rome according to Christian tradition, hence his name *Martyr*, meaning "witness" in

Greek. He wrote two apologies and the famous *Dialogue with Trypho*. As Plato had defended Socrates 500 years earlier, so did Justin attempt to justify his belief as a Christian and, like Socrates, failed to save his life. The thrust of Justin's argument, both in his apologies and in the *Dialogue*, is that the Bible proves Christianity right and sensible readers should realize that the prophets of Israel foretold the coming of Jesus. Justin's writings contain many biblical exegeses and attempt to show that Jewish traditions predated Greek ones. The first apology offers several examples. In a discussion of free will, Justin quotes the following teaching: "And the holy Spirit of prophecy taught us this, telling us by Moses that spoke thus to the man first created: 'Behold, before thy face are good and evil: choose the good'" (Chapter 44). Further on, Justin claims that when Plato argues in The Republic, Book X, that "the blame is his who chooses and God is blameless," he is merely imitating Moses, who lived long before him. Note, however, that the passage Justin presumes to quote is not from the Bible at all. The closest biblical text, to which Justin's annotators point, is Deuteronomy 30:15–19: "See, I have set before thee this day life and good, and death and evil...therefore choose life." Justin, however, claimed that this was God's command to the "man first created," whereas the Bible offers no evidence of such a command to Adam. Where did Justin find this command? I believe we can view this as a classic anti-gnostic exegesis. Justin claims that God commanded His first creature to choose the good, as this God sought to help Adam and direct him on the right path.

The timing of divine revelation was a major challenge to both Christianity and Judaism. Pagans argued it was inconceivable that God, the Creator of the Universe, would bestow His grace on one nation alone. Why, in the words of Julian the Apostate, "he even looked on for myriads, or if you prefer, for thousands of years" (*Against the Galilaeans*, 106d p. 343). Justin's response to this kind of an attack was not late in coming. Justin emphasizes that, because Christ was the first creature, the *logos*, all those who lived before his revelation but acted rationally, following the *logos*, are considered Christians. R. Simeon b. Yohai's homily, mentioned earlier, is now worth considering in its entirety: "The Holy One, blessed be He, measured all the nations and found none worthy of receiving the Torah except Israel, and the Holy One, blessed be He, measured all the generations and found none worthy of receiving the Torah except the generation of the desert" (*Leviticus Rabbah* 13:2).

Justin and his contemporary R. Simeon b. Yohai contend with the question of the timing of revelation. Justin claims that revelation was delayed, but the generations preceding it suffered no loss and were able to share in the divine essence of the first creature. R. Simeon's answer is more assertive: he holds that the Holy One, blessed be He, chose the only appropriate timing, with wisdom and understanding. One should not question the virtues and decisions of the Creator, according to R. Simeon, and this question can only be answered at the level of pure faith.

Justin and the Church attempted to appropriate the Torah of the Jews for several reasons. First, the Church believed itself to be the only body capable of decoding the biblical message accurately. According to the Christians, the Jews were unable to understand their own Torah. Rather, the Torah and the Prophets were important to Christianity to prove that the coming of Christ was the fulfillment of age-old prophecies. At the same time, the Church relied on the Bible and its Jewish origins to ward off the Roman claim that Christians worship "new gods that came newly up"—a new invention of people who hate humanity (*misanthropia*). On grounds of politics as well as faith, then, the Church attempted to appropriate Jewish Scripture in its entirety, while engaged in a stubborn struggle with both Jews and gnostics over its interpretation.

Neither Judaism nor Christianity, then, attempted to hide the views of their rivals. Instead, they contested them, and their controversies have been preserved in the Midrash, the Talmuds, as well as in many Christian works. Both religions fought strenuously against the gnostic threat, while arguing with one another. Insufficient awareness of the pagan claims against Christianity and Judaism may make the deeper layers of these two religious traditions inaccessible. Furthermore, insensitivity to the gnostic menace threatening both religions may obscure the true intention of a homily, as I tried to show regarding R. Nathan. Only when biblical exegesis is considered within a broader literary context will the rabbis' beliefs, as well as those of their opponents, emerge clearly.

2

The Core of Contention:
"They Are Not Israel...We Are Israel"

When we attempt to delineate the parameters of an encounter between two religions we must first consider separately the internal structure of each one: its values, ideas, and practices. This description will not suffice either, unless we can determine the balance between these three components and their relative importance.[1] Whereas in one religion thought and concepts are more important than praxis, in another "intention" counts for less and practice is decisive. Only after conducting a survey of this type can the comparison proceed.

This is also the case when one religion claims to be the heir of the other, draws from the same sources, adopts the same ancestral myths, and presumes, in fact, to be *the* true religion, arguing that the other has lost its identity and authenticity. Whether the pretenders to the crown have their roots in the first religion or whether they are outsiders does not matter. Their claim is that the legacy which has so far been understood and practiced in a specific way is now the patrimony of a greater and more expert interpreter, who holds the true keys to its understanding and fulfillment.

This is the beginning of a theoretical survey charting the relations between two religions in general and between early Christianity and the religion of Israel in particular, a task that may be hard, or even impossible, for one person to carry out thoroughly. I will not attempt to describe here the content and the structure of the two religions. Instead, I will confine myself to the portrayal of one decisive encounter; namely, the battle over biblical exegesis, a crucial issue in the rivalry between Christians and Jews. One of the chief arguments adduced by Christians was that Jews had not understood the Bible properly. The most radical formulation of this approach is the well known saying by Augustine, one of the most famous figures among the Church Fathers, who lived at the end of the fourth and beginning of the fifth centuries. Augustine compares the role of the Jews to that of a blind man, who lights up the road for others with his torch but cannot see the light himself.[2] In these terms then, the Jew attests to the truths of the Bible without understanding them. I show below how Christianity attempted to support this view. The most poignant formulation of the Christians' claim to the true understanding of the Bible is their demand to be defined as "the true Israel." This argument appears early in Christian literature, but is mentioned in rabbinic literature in midrashim edited only at a relatively late stage, such as *Tanhuma* (*Ki Tisa*):[3] "Because the Holy One, blessed be He, foresaw that a time would come when the nations of the world would translate the Torah, read it in Greek and then say: 'We are Israel...'" The Midrash then, clearly identifies the element aspiring to dispossess the Jews of their biblical legacy: Gentiles who translate Scripture into Greek and pretend to be Israel. The answer to the claim raised in this midrash will concern us here.

A preliminary question is in place here: Is there any evidence at all indicating that Jews were aware of this argument from the start of the period we are considering, even if they did not mention it explicitly? During the second century, as before, Christians publicly stated that they were the true Israel, that only they could interpret Scripture adequately, and that Jews no longer had a share in it because they had refused to understand its true meaning. Let us examine their claim in Justin's formulation and then return to consider the extent to which early Jewish sources show any awareness of it.

Justin's *Dialogue with Trypho* is a crucial source in the Christian-Jewish debate. It was apparently written in Rome around the year 160 C.E.,[4] the "Usha" period in rabbinic Palestine. Trypho, the Jewish representative in the dialogue, asks: "What, then? Are you Israel? And speaks He such things [the biblical prophecies mentioned before] of you?"

And Justin answers: "As therefore from the one man Jacob, who was surnamed Israel, all your nation has been called Jacob and Israel; so we from Christ, who begat us unto God, like Jacob, and Israel, and Judah, and Joseph, and David, are called and are the true sons of God, and keep the commandments of Christ" (Chapter 123). "You are the children of the Lord your God" (Deuteronomy 14:1), says Moses to the people of Israel in the desert. And R. Akiva, an older contemporary of Justin, returns to this motif: "Beloved are Israel, for they were called children of God; still greater was the love in that they were called children of God" (Avot 3:14).[5] In R. Akiva's method, Israel are not beloved simply because they were created in God's image, like all human beings ("Beloved is man, for he was created in the image [of God]"), but they are especially beloved—as they were called children. According to Justin's method, however, the children now beloved are those who observe the commands of the Messiah. Justin elaborates the view of Paul (Galatians 3:7), who had addressed gentile Christians as the "children of Abraham." R. Akiva's precious vessel, the Torah, was replaced by "the commands of the Messiah" (foremost among them faith), which entitled the Christians to the names of Israel-Jacob and children of God.

This claim appears in explicit terms in the *Tanhuma* passage quoted previously, but is found in an even earlier source:

A parable. To what is this similar? The straw, the chaff and the stubble engaged in a controversy. This one says: "For my sake was the land sown" and that one says: "For my sake was the land sown." Said the wheat to them: "Wait until the harvest comes and then we shall see for whom the field was sown." When harvest time came and all go to the threshing floor, the landowner went out to thresh, the chaff was scattered to the wind; he took the straw and threw it to the ground; he took the stubble and burnt it; he took the wheat and piled it into a stack and everybody kissed it. In like manner the nations, these say: "We are Israel and for our sake was the world created." And these say: "We are Israel and for our sake was the world created." Says Israel to them: "Wait until the day of the Holy One, blessed be He, and we shall know for whom was the world created, as it is written 'For, behold, that day is coming; it burns like a furnace' (Malachi 3:19) and it is written

'Thou shalt fan them, and the wind shall carry then away' (Isaiah 41:16), but, as for Israel we are told: 'And thou shalt rejoice in the Lord, and shalt glory in the Holy One of Israel' (ibid.)." (*Midrash on the Song of Songs* 7:3)

Here again is a source that explicitly relates to the claim of the "nations," and disputes it: "Wait"—the day will still come for the Jews to prove that *they* are Israel, "the children of God." An even earlier version of this homily is preserved in *Genesis Rabbah*, end of section 83, and is particularly interesting. I quote only the moral of the story: "In like manner, Israel and the nations have a controversy, these say 'for our sake was the world created' and these say 'for our sake.' Israel say, the hour will come and you will see [in the future] 'Thou shalt fan them and the wind shall carry them away' (Isaiah 41:16), but Israel 'And thou shalt rejoice in the Lord, and shalt glory in the Holy One of Israel' (ibid.)." The earlier midrash, then, does not explicitly allude to the Christian argument, but merely hints to it: "for our sake was the world created." Only in *Tanhuma*, a later work, are the two elements combined—"we are Israel," and the Scripture's translation into Greek. The merger of these two elements is what enables the sure identification of the "nations" as the Christians. But should not the later source be seen as an accurate and faithful interpretation of the previous ones? The study of another source (*PT Peah* 2:6) will show that, definitely by the fourth century, if not before, the rabbis were contending with the Christian claim.

The context of this source is a discussion of the concept *halakha le-Moshe mi-Sinai* [a law given to Moses at Sinai], which appears in the mishnah ad locum. The Talmud goes on to clarify the relationship between rabbinic law—the Oral Law—and the revelation at Sinai. Is the Written Law preferable to the Oral Law or vice versa, or are they both perhaps of equal value? Several answers are given to this question, all quite different, although all rest on scriptural exegesis. The central verse, which opens the discussion, is from Exodus 34:27—"for according to [*al pi*; literally, "by the mouth"] these words have I made a covenant with thee and with Israel." This is expounded by one *amora* as pointing to the primacy of the Oral Law—in other words, this is the essence of the covenant and in his formulation—"[the words] in the mouth are beloved."

The second topic of discussion in this talmudic passage is the important one. The verse expounded here (Hosea 8:12) requires clarification: "Though I write for him the great things of my Torah, they are reckoned a strange thing." R. Avin expounds it as follows: "Said R. Avin, 'Had I written for you the bulk of my [orally transmitted] Torah, would they [the Jews] not be considered as foreigners? [For] what [is the difference] between them and the Gentiles? These bring forth their books and these bring forth their books; these bring forth *diftera* [skins] and these bring forth *diftera.'"*[6] As mentioned, the context of this passage in the Palestinian Talmud is a profound and comprehensive discussion of the status of the Oral Law, which concludes with the famous saying "even that which a learned student someday in the future will recite before his master was told to Moses at Sinai." It seems clear that R. Avin also believes that the Oral Law rather than Scripture is what marks Israel as unique. The full version of the "later" midrash follows, and I will return to sum up the passage from the Palestinian Talmud in its light. This early passage conceals what the later midrash is prepared to disclose. This version of the midrash appears in *Pesikta Rabbati* (*Piska* 5):

> Said R. Judah bar Shalom: Moses asked that the Mishnah be committed to writing. But the Holy One, blessed be He, foresaw that the nations would translate the Torah, read it in Greek, and say…"We are Israel," "We are the children of the Lord." Now the scales are balanced. The Holy One, blessed be He, will then say to the nations… "I only know he who possesses my mysteries, he is my child." They said to Him, "And what are your mysteries?" Said He to them, "That is the Mishnah."

According to R. Judah bar Shalom, the nations and Israel are equal pretenders to the crown ("the scales are balanced");[7] ostensibly, then, no verdict is possible. For this fourth-century exegete then, the threat the Church posed in the form of the Septuagint was very real indeed. Only the Oral Law gave the Jews an advantage or, more accurate, only the Oral Law defined the true, authentic identity of the children of God. It is very tempting to emphasize the word *mystery*, which appears in its Greek form, *mysterin*, in the original Hebrew. Mystery religions had swept the Roman world in rabbinic times, and this could actually be an attempt to establish an image of Judaism as a mystery religion, its mystery being the Oral Law. This could also explain the unparalleled role of oral study in the rabbis' view. Lieberman hinted in this direction when expounding on this source.[8]

Although the last hypothesis appears to me essentially correct, I wonder whether the reading of *mysterin*, though preserved in all the manuscripts, is correct.[9] Often, in similar contexts, the word here used is not *mysterin* but *sementerin*. *Sementerin*, meaning seal in Greek, appears precisely in those parables where the Midrash deals with questions of identity.[10]

Leaving philological musings aside, the intention of this homily is absolutely clear. The Mishnah, the Oral Law, identifies Israel as the children of God and marks them as unique. We can now return to the Palestinian Talmud. When R. Avin, who precedes R. Judah bar Shalom by one or two generations, says "[For] what [is the difference] between us and the Gentiles?" he is addressing the same problem: The Torah is written and open to anyone who wishes to read it. As Lieberman says:[11] "In this homily the Christians are portrayed as producing the *Septuagint* in the form of books and *diftera*...because, according to the Rabbis, they wished to stress that in regard to the Torah they were on a par with the Jews. They have the same books in the same form as the Jews have." We saw, then, that the two earlier sources—from the Palestinian Talmud and from *Genesis Rabbah*—do not mention the Christian argument explicitly, although they do hint to it. In contrast, the later version of the homilies explains the hidden meaning and fully brings it out.

Let us return to Lieberman's previous point, when he compared the Oral Law to the mystery religions. I believe this issue should be related to the strict ban placed on the writing of books of *aggadah* (*PT, Shabbat* 16:1): "This *aggada*, he who writes it down has no share [in the world to come]; he who preaches it should be burned, and he who hears it will receive no reward." This surprising statement is ascribed to one of the foremost aggadists, R. Joshuah b. Levi, who asserts that only once in his lifetime did he look at a book of *aggada*. Indeed, *tannaim* had already ruled that even the exegesis of Scripture was to be done orally, as we learn from the *Tosefta* (Shabbat 13:1): "Even though they have said, 'We do not read in Holy Scriptures [on the sabbath]' but we do teach [*shonim*] them and we expound [*dorshim*] them. And if one needs to check something, he takes the Scripture and checks it." The *Tosefta* offers a lenient view here. Whereas the *Mishnah* (Shabbath 16:1) absolutely forbids the reading of Scripture "lest they negate the *beit-hamidrash* [house of study]," the *Tosefta* limits this ban to reading only and allows "to teach" and "to expound." For our purposes, the point is that even this lenient view assumes that Scripture is to be expounded without looking at the biblical text, and so, a fortiori, they certainly would not allow the study of books of *aggadah*. Thus, the *tannaim* stressed that, even on the sabbath, which was the central day of study for the people, the study of Scripture should only be done orally! A quick glimpse at the written text, for purposes of checking a reference, would be allowed. These and other sources clearly show that *aggada* books were available, which aroused bitter opposition by some rabbis.[12] Additional evidence of the existence of such books is offered later, where Jerome tells of a Jew sneaking in at night to bring him books of the Hebrews.[13] The Midrash, as well as the *Mishnah*, were to be guarded carefully lest their contents leak out or, worse still, fall into the hands of the exegetical competitors.

Several reasons were adduced for the Christians' desire to procure the title *Israel*. First and foremost was the historical fact that the new religion had originated among Jews and, at its outset, had spread among them and seen itself as continuing Judaism. The historical reason is not the main one, however, especially after the repudiation of the Jews and the mission to the gentiles. Clearly, the fact that Christianity had no legitimate status in the Roman empire was sufficient reason for the Christians' desire to remain under the aegis of Judaism, which enjoyed this enviable legal status. The perception of Christians as worshippers of "new gods that came newly up" (Deuteronomy 32:17), who had not followed in the ways of their fathers, gave the Roman authorities a valid reason for persecuting the new religion.[14] For Christians, adherence to Jewish roots certainly entailed an advantage, enabling them to claim a very old and legitimate lineage. These claims notwithstanding, Christians were persecuted during these centuries, and Justin himself died as a martyr. Beyond the historical reason and the political explanations, however, I believe we must also say that Christians believed with perfect faith that the believers in their Messiah were, indeed, the real Jews and the true Israel of their time, and those who denied this were "transgressors." The combined strength of these three arguments turned the battle over Scripture, Israel's quintessential legacy, into a matter of life and death. This struggle, as it comes to the fore in different Christian writings, is described below.

Describing this hermeneutical controversy is a complex and intricate endeavor. Early Christianity soon leaves the confines of Palestine and, in its missions to the nations of the world, uses a variety of languages. For the Christians, the missions themselves are a stage in the fulfillment of Malachi's prophecy "and in every place incense is burnt and sacrifices are offered to my name, and a pure offering: for my name is great among the nations, says the Lord of hosts" (1:11) (Justin Martyr, *Dialogue* Ch. 41). Relying on the swift spread of their religion, Christians will claim, as early as the second century, that they are Israel and have fulfilled this prophecy. The problems affecting the inquiry into this expansion are obvious. A Greek-writing Christian in Palestine, living in close proximity to Jewish centers, differs significantly from his learned colleague who thinks and writes in Latin and is far removed in time and place from the Jewish hub of creativity. Both of them, moreover, are quite different from the Christian writing in Syriac, a language similar to the Aramaic spoken by Palestinian Jewry, as well as the prominent Jewish community of Antioch, in Syria.

A second reason making this description of the Christian communities so complex is related to the first: in addition to languages, different exegetic and philosophic schools, as well as theological approaches, developed in the various areas and decisively affected local creativity. Internal theological disputes also constitute important material for the understanding of Church exegesis. It is beyond the scope of this work to introduce the reader to the abstract theological discussions on the essence of God and the relationship between the elements of the trinity.

A third reason that makes this portrayal of the battle over Scripture so complex is that the Christians developed several genres of written exegesis. At least six prominent ones can be counted:

1. Classic exegetical works.
2. Homiletic works that are, more or less, stenographic transcripts of Church sermons.
3. Apologetics, monographs in defense of the Christian religion meant to ward off attacks by pagans, Jews, and gnostics.
4. Anthologies of homilies on single verses, organized to create a running commentary on a specific biblical book.
5. Notes from classes given at the academy of a specific Christian thinker.
6. Songs and ritual poems, which are replete with exegeses.

Several other genres—histories, letters, stories of martyrdom, and so forth—also include biblical comments written in the Church during these years.

These three elements—the language of the work, its geographic and intellectual milieu, and the literary form of the exegesis—all hamper attempts at a uniform description of Christian biblical exegeses.

On the Jewish side, creativity during these years was more focused both in time and place and, quite surprising, in genre. In fact, only one (or perhaps two) "styles" of exegetical works have survived: "midrashim" that include the *midrash halakha* of the tannaitic period (until the middle of the third century), and the *midreshei aggadah* of the *amoraim*, which were edited, in the form known to us, between the end of the fourth century and the Moslem conquest at the beginning of the seventh. The tendency is to distinguish between exegetic and homiletic *midreshei aggadah*. The exegetic midrash follows a specific biblical book verse by verse and comments on each one (as is the case in *Genesis Rabbah*); the homiletic midrash presents more distinct and integrated material on a specific subject and does not deal exhaustively with all verses in their order of appearance in a given biblical book (as is the case in *Leviticus Rabbah*).

Unquestionably, in homiletic midrashim, ideas are developed more extensively and thoroughly, but the basic exegetic kernel in both midrashic genres—the exegetic and the homiletic—is very similar and perhaps identical.[15]

Jews and Christians battled over the question, Who is the true Israel? Both religions clung to the Bible in Hebrew or Greek and interpreted it, each according to its own method. In the debates between them, the Bible was at the center: Whereas the Oral Law was unique to the Jews, Christianity saw its singularity in its belief in Jesus as the Messiah and his grace to humanity. Within this context, each of these religions turned to interpret the Bible and persuade each other, their own believers, and the pagan onlookers that it was the true Israel.

3

On Oratory and Writing:
Exegete, Preacher, and Audience in Antiquity

The orator, the *rhetor* of the ancient world, sought to achieve three aims through his speeches: to persuade, to educate, and to amuse.[1] The skilled *rhetor* knew how to adapt his speech to the audience and the issue at hand. In the study of Christian preaching, much attention has recently been devoted to an attempt to estimate the character of the audience by the standard of the sermon.[2] For instance, to judge by that most masterful of preachers, Gregory of Nyssa in Asia Minor, he addressed a highly educated audience. Indeed, his linguistic flamboyancy has been severely criticized by scholars, and he has been described as afflicted with the disease of sophists, who untiringly scatter words to the winds.

Proving that reality truly was as it appears to be reflected in the written texts available to us, however, is not easy: Who will guarantee that this particular preacher did, indeed, deliver his live sermon as written? Might this not be a polished literary revision, abiding by all rules of rhetorical etiquette and intended for an educated and believing public or even for a limited group of Church dignitaries and preachers? If so, the actual sermon may well have been much simpler than the product before us. Although the question is raised here regarding Christian writings presented as homilies, it is just as relevant in regard to rabbinic midrashim.[3]

Christian writings on the Bible, as was mentioned in Chapter 2, have been preserved in several forms and genres. Since my concern here is with patristics rather than with early Christianity proper, I begin my review from the second century and continue until the beginning of the sixth. Second century Christian writings are quite diverse and include, among others, briefs in defense of religion known as *apologia*. This is an ancient literary tradition, the most famous apology in the ancient world certainly that of Plato. This period in Church history is known, because of these writings by Christians, as the era of the apologists. One of the major and most celebrated apologies is the *Dialogue with Trypho* by Justin Martyr, which is discussed more extensively in the next chapter. This work, presented as a dialogue between a Jew and a Christian, is marked by the tension that characterized the relations between the early Church and the Jews concerning the true interpretation of the Bible.

During the third century, the Church witnessed the emergence of one of its most creative and prolific figures throughout the ancient period—Origen of Alexandria (c. 180–253). His works comprise classic biblical exegeses, as well as collections containing transcriptions of the public sermons he delivered in Caesarea around 230 C.E.[4] Origen's erudition, together with his love and devotion to the Bible, "which includes nothing that is not useful," yielded fruit and spurred a growing concern with biblical exegesis among his followers, who championed the allegorical interpretation of the Bible, as well as his opponents. Although rudimentary attempts at biblical exegesis are clearly discernible as early as the second century, Origen must be credited with the impetus given to biblical studies in later generations.

Didymus the Blind of Alexandria (313–398), one of Origen's spiritual heirs, even left notes from Didymus' classes on Bible teaching at Didymus' academy. These notes were found in a cache of his writings discovered in the 1941 papyrus find in Tura, Egypt. The documents are particularly interesting, as they afford us a glimpse into the live dialogue between a teacher and his students—we see the teacher fielding questions, departing from his planned schedule, and so forth.[5] The "School of Antioch, " to which we alluded when discussing Origen's opponents, must be mentioned here. This school recoiled from what it considered the exaggerated reliance on allegory and typology characteristic of the Alexandrian school. An allegorical exegesis is one exposing another dimension or a different message in the interpreted text, beyond that disclosed at first glance. The word *allegory* is itself composed of two Greek words meaning "other speaking." Through this device, words are turned into symbols or types (which is Greek for "figure," hence the term *typology*), conveying a deeper message. These approaches are illustrated in the following chapters. Note that allegorical interpretation had been well known for several centuries B.C.E. at least as a tool for understanding Homer, and also had supporters and opponents. As for the allegorical interpretation of the Bible, Origen was also preceded by two great Alexandrians, one Jewish (Philo) and the other Christian (Clement), both of whom Origen mentions by name.[6] Because of his intellectual and interpretive powers, however, Origen came to personify the method and be seen as its most accomplished practitioner. Thus, as Origen's death approached, the men of Antioch voiced their vehement opposition to his exaggerated allegorical interpretation; instead, they favored an approach called *theoria* that, although not altogether free of allegory, attaches greater validity to the historical context of biblical books and is less inclined to read so many verses as heralding the coming of Jesus.[7]

This short survey will end with Procopius of Gaza (475–536), who seems to have been the first Church figure to collect various interpretations into anthologies known as *catenae* or *eklogae*. The form of these anthologies was familiar to him, a qualified rhetor, from similar writings in classical literature, and he adopted it when collecting exegeses of biblical books by different authors. Although Procopius' work has been described as a sad development, attesting to a decline in creativity, this is not necessarily the case.[8] In fact, we could say, and I believe we should, that Procopius' outstanding feat was to produce an exegetical work, containing named sources, that includes some interpretations and spurns others. The criterion for measuring creativity in this case, then, is in the assemblage of exegeses and in his choice of authors.

So far, I have reviewed the main styles of exegeses and *drashot* prevalent in the Greek-speaking East, during a period roughly parallel to that extending from the Mishnah to the editing of amoraic midrashim (135–535). I have tried to present a broad spectrum of the Christian writings and Christian personalities that should be considered when attempting to compare Christian works and rabbinic midrashim. To focus the study, I have limited it mainly to Church Fathers active in Palestine and its vicinity who wrote in Greek during the times of the *tannaim* and the *amoraim*—

beginning with Justin Martyr, who was born in Shechem, Palestine, in the second century, through Origen, who was active in Caesarea until the middle of the third century, and ending with Procopius of Gaza, at the end of the fifth century. We may assume that these figures were especially sensitive to exegetical claims advanced by Jews and that they applied themselves to becoming a true and persuasive alternative that, by virtue of their interpretations, could claim a lead role in the understanding of the Bible. We noted that Origen was sensitive to the derision shown by Jews to the illiteracy of Christians in Hebrew (regarding the Passover). Instead of concentrating on the Christian variety of speculative hermeneutics on the essence of divinity, I have focused on exegeses that, among others, strike back at the two rival forces perceived by the Church as explicit and immediate theological threats—on the one hand, the Jews, and on the other hand, the gnostics.[9]

Some scholars argue that, during its first 300 years, the main hermeneutical effort of Christian exegetes was devoted to steering a middle course between the Jewish and the gnostic interpretations of the Bible. Gnosticism was a trend within religion claiming superior and special knowledge (from the Greek *gnosis* = knowledge). Scholars were divided as to whether this trend originated among Jews and then spread to Christianity or vice versa. I side with those who see in Judaism the breeding ground of Gnosis.[10] At any event, some gnostics close to Christianity claimed that the Creator reflected in the Bible is different from the God of love revealed in the New Testament. They described the God of Israel as cruel, as the creator of a flawed world wherein the forces of darkness overpower the forces of light. Only the gnostic, by virtue of special knowledge, can prevail and unite with the hidden, vanished God of love. Christianity split into several groups during the first centuries of its existence, which were at odds regarding the holiness of Jewish Scriptures in general and even regarding the holiness of some New Testament books. One of the most prominent figures was Marcion, who presumed to be able to distinguish the true passages about the God of love in the New Testament and the dross that he saw as belonging to the God of Israel, which had insinuated itself into the New Testament.

In principle, I had intended to focus on documents written in two languages—the Greek of the Church and the Hebrew/Aramaic of Judaism. Even this was not an easy decision, but any attempt to trace mutual influences and patterns of cross-fertilization must be sensitive to the technical terminology as well as to the biblical text used by the homilist. Although it is generally true that the Greek Fathers of the Church used the Septuagint, we may safely assume that other translations were also available to them. Some of the Fathers even took the trouble of consulting the Hebrew original. As soon as we move to the Latin versions of the Bible, however, or to the writings of Greek Fathers that have only been preserved in their Latin translation, research becomes much more complex.

I have not abided by this principle because it would have entailed too great a loss: two figures crucial to my endeavor—Origen, whose writings have been preserved mainly in Latin translation, and Jerome, who wrote in Latin—would have been left out. Although some of Origen's most important works have been preserved in their original Greek, all of Jerome' writings are in Latin. Jerome, who lived in a Bethlehem monastery at the end of the fourth century, is known as the author of the Vulgate, the Latin translation of the Bible that he embarked on because of his belief in the truth of the Hebrew original. He was forced to translate the Bible anew, so that the translation would accurately reflect the source. Jerome had contacts with Jewish teachers and even included many of their commentaries in his works.

Thus far this is the domain of the study. Another area of Christian creativity directly related to our subject remains to be explored, but I review it only briefly for the reasons just mentioned. I refer to the Fathers who wrote in Syriac and lived on the borders of Palestine. Ephraem Syrus and his colleagues deserve a separate inquiry, and some studies have indeed been concerned with this topic. The poetic-exegetical works of Ephraem Syrus, however, cannot be ignored, and I review them later.

The abundance of genres in Christian writings, of which only some have been mentioned, is conspicuously evident from this short review. But relying on this material for evidence concerning the question we asked at the opening of this chapter—how to

separate the live sermon from the literary exegesis—will not be
easy. The comparison between these works and Jewish Midrash, to
which we now turn, will, I believe, enable a reappraisal of Jewish
creativity.

Until recently, tradition and scholarly research shared a
perception of midrashim as popular works.[11] Rashi's commentary
on the wonderful homily found in the Babylonian Talmud
(Shabbat 30b) is, perhaps, the most poignant expression of this
view. A question is raised there as to whether it is permitted to put
out a candle burning next to a sick person's bed on the sabbath to
allow this person to sleep. The homily reads: "a candle is called a
candle and the soul of man is called a candle; better it is that the
candle of flesh and blood be extinguished before the candle of the
Holy One, blessed be He." The source of the motif that regards the
individual's soul as God's candle is the verse "The spirit of man is
the candle of the Lord" (Proverbs 20:27), and the rabbis use it in
several homilies. Rashi, the greatest medieval commentator, feels
obliged to point out that the homily is not the source of the
halakha that allows one to put out the candle for a sleeping patient
but, rather, was introduced "'to spice up' the ruling with an
appealing *aggada*, since women and the uneducated (*amei ha'arets*)
would come to hear the sermon, and the preachers would have to
draw their attention (lit.—draw their hearts)." Rashi relies here on
a formulation found in the *Mekhilta de-Rabbi Ishmael*, where an
exegesis on the manna in the desert describes it as "the coriander
seed (heb.-'gad').... R. Eleazar of Modi'im says: 'It was like the
words of *aggada*, which draw the hearts of people'" (Vayass'a, 5).[12]
Note the transition between the *Mekhilta*, "draw the hearts of
people," and Rashi, who sees it as appealing to women and to the
uneducated.

Two factors weigh against this approach to Midrash. The first
is that the gap between oral and written homilies must be considered. Even if some homilies were articulated in public, their
wording as is now available in midrashic collections is, without
doubt, a literary, written adaptation, which does not reproduce
exactly what was said in synagogue sermons. As preachers have
often reworked oral sermons into a literary form when their time
came to be written, the same seems true regarding our classic

midrashim. Second, even if we say that written homilies are close to their oral, public version, remember that audiences obviously varied;[13] the community in Caesarea was not the same as that in Tiberias, and surely differed from that in Sakhnin, and all these communities are certainly different from that of the students at the *beth-midrash*, who studied the weekly portion or some other book of the Bible. Some of the midrashim embedded in our anthologies reflect the dialogue that the rabbis conducted among themselves, perhaps within the walls of the house of study. The study of midrash from this perspective, however, is only just beginning, and I try to further discussion of this question in the following chapters, by way of a comparison with Christian works.

We have limited our field of study to Palestinian midrashim. The 400 years covered in this study, beginning at 135 C.E., encompass the period during which the *midreshei halakha*, as well as the "classic" *midreshei aggadah* of the *amoraim*, are assumed to have been written. These range from the "older" aggadic midrashim—*Genesis Rabbah, Leviticus Rabbah*, and *Pesikta de-Rav Kahana*—to some of the midrashim on the Scrolls. As a basis for our comparison, then, we have midrashim on the books of the Torah—at least one on each—and on some of the Scrolls. We have also included a chapter on a midrash putatively dated about a hundred years later—*Ecclesiastes Rabbah*. The character of *Ecclesiastes Rabbah* as an ancient "anthology" drawing from various sources invited comparison with a parallel phenomenon we encounter in the Church from the sixth century. A further reason for including *Ecclesiastes Rabbah* is the need to illustrate the antiquity of part of the material inlaid in this midrash, purported to be a later work, by comparing it to Christian works whose "early" dating is proven and that include traditions these works identify as "Jewish." Although I am not the first one to point this out,[14] I believe this topic merits consideration in this book. The last reason for this choice is my continued interest in the history and the sources of *Ecclesiastes Rabbah*. (I did not, however, consider it appropriate to discuss the problem of the *Tanhumah Yelamedenu* midrashim in this framework.)

Midrashic creativity will be found to include suggestions of poetry, some limited vestiges of public sermons, and "exegesis" proper—the trademark of Midrash. Exegeses at times assume the form of a story while, at others, they infer from a remote verse in an attempt to illuminate the verse at hand. Furthermore, larger units will impress observers as the product of a conscious editing of minute homiletic fragments. In the following chapters, I focus on the difference between Midrash and its Christian counterparts. To a large extent, hermeneutical methods are shared by these two traditions, as well as by their cultural environment. Nevertheless, the very compilation involved in the midrashic anthologies that have reached us, and the rabbis' exclusive reliance on this literary genre, distinguish their work from that of the Church, as well as from that of the surroundings. I tend to interpret this literary fact as a creative isolation from the surrounding milieu. This detachment worked even more effectively in those Jewish circles that cautiously refrained from writing down their homilies, scornful of "books of *aggada*." In the following chapters, I attempt to support this perception of the midrashic endeavor.

Although the broad range of genres used by Christians may be a natural corollary of the use of Greek and Latin in their writings, it may also be a prominent indication of Christian proselytizing intentions.

4

The Exegetical Debate: Justin Martyr and the *Dialogue with Trypho the Jew*

Justin Martyr became famous in the Christian world for two types of works. The first are the defense briefs (apologia in Greek), where he refutes Roman charges against Christians. The second has no specific title and includes only one work—*Dialogue with Trypho.*[1] The *Dialogue* complements the apologia in turning from defense to offense and providing a powerful indictment of Judaism, of the Jewish teachers, and of their biblical exegeses. The *Dialogue* comprises the main Christian allegations against Judaism and affords us a clear picture of biblical interpretation in the age of the apologists. The *Dialogue* makes an even more significant contribution, because Justin quotes the biblical exegeses of "the 'sages' (*didaskaloi* in Greek) of the Jews."[2] The study of these exegeses, as such and in comparison with rabbinic midrashim found in tannaitic and amoraic collections, is of great interest.

By his own testimony, Justin was born in Flavia Neapolis, which is Shechem, apparently to a family of settlers of Greco-Roman ancestry.[3] The first eight chapters of his *Dialogue* describe Justin's spiritual voyage until he acknowledged Christian truth. Some scholars strongly doubt the authenticity of this description and view it as an imitation of a well-known literary topos.[4] In any event, evidence attesting to Justin's martyrdom, which earned him the sobriquet "witness" (*martyrus* in Greek), dates as far back as the end of the second century. According to most accounts, Justin died around the year 165 C.E. and is assumed to have been born at the beginning of the second century. Scholars believe that the *Dialogue* was written in the fifties of the second century, about ten years before his death. In its present form, Justin writes a letter to his friend Marcus with an account of a dialogue Justin had conducted with the Jew Trypho, "a refugee from the Judean war."

The 142 chapters of the book can be divided into four sections:

1. Chapters 1–9. The "chance" meeting between Justin and Trypho wherein Justin recounts his diverse philosophical encounters, culminating in the revelation of the "old man," who taught him that Christianity is the only true philosophy.
2. Chapters 10–47: Justin "proves" to Trypho, that the laws given to the Jews are not incumbent on Christians.
3. Chapters 48–107: Jesus is the Messiah.
4. Chapters 108–142: Christians are the true Israel.[5]

It needs to be emphasized that the arguments and proofs Justin plies upon his Jewish interlocutor take the form of biblical exegeses. At times, Justin even takes the trouble of quoting the "Jewish" version of the Bible, as if thereby saying that the Jew Trypho must concede the truth of his homilies. One of his main goals in this treatise is to prove to the Jews, represented by Trypho and his companions, that the rabbis had failed at the task of biblical exegesis and persuade them that the Christian interpretation, received through the grace of Christ and his apostles, is the true one. A further concern of some Christian biblical exegesis at the time was the refutation of the gnostic argument that the Jewish Bible is the creation of a bad god, the demiurge. Therefore, the gnostics rejected the Jewish Bible altogether, while the Jews rejected the Christian-messianic interpretation of Scripture endorsed by Justin and his colleagues.[6] Justin's answer was that the Christian exegesis is the only true interpretation of the Bible, which heralded and foretold the events to come in Jesus' times. I will cite several examples of Justin's approach and of the "answers" given by Trypho and his companions in the *Dialogue*, and then go on to contrast them with documented rabbinic homilies on the same topics and verses. It is essential to begin with a sketch of the characters taking part in the dialogue and their literary roles.

The Jew Trypho presents himself as the disciple of a philosopher named Corinthus, who, among other things, taught him that whenever he sees anyone walking in the market arrayed in a philosopher's dress, he must accost him and engage him in useful dialogue (1:2).[7] These were the circumstances of the encounter between Trypho and Justin. This is not a dialogue between equals—the Jew Trypho is the disciple, while the Christian Justin is portrayed as a highly experienced philosopher, educated in all the important schools. Indeed, Trypho identifies himself to Justin in the following manner: "'Trypho,' says he, 'I am called; and I am a Hebrew of the circumcision, and having escaped from the war lately carried on there, I am spending my days in Greece, and chiefly at Corinth'" (1:3). After confirming that he was deeply impressed by his reading of the "so-called Gospel," Trypho casts doubts on whether a mortal is capable of keeping its precepts (10:2). This opening gives a clear indication of Justin's tendency to create an image of a Jew open to the Christian gospel. A most interesting phenomenon deserving attention is that almost all the teachings of the "Jewish sages" (some of which have clear parallels in rabbinic literature) are actually quoted by Justin, although we would expect the Jew to be the spokesman of classic Jewish homilies and arguments. In this dialogue, however, Justin's motivation for not using Trypho as the mouthpiece of the Jewish homilies was carefully designed. Several other aspects of Trypho's role need to be considered before going into the reason for this curious fact.

Trypho plays an active role only until Chapter 90, about 60 percent of the book.[8] His main task is to ask leading questions, which Justin answers thoroughly and skillfully. Trypho does not hide that he is highly impressed by Justin and by the force of his arguments (63:1), and when Justin claims that the leaders of the Jews changed some verses in Scripture, Trypho has no better answer than, "Whether [or not] the rulers of the people have erased any portion of the Scriptures…God knows" (73:5). Toward the end of the *Dialogue* Trypho even repeats a question, so that Justin might "exhibit the same proof to these men" (Trypho's friends—123:7). Only two or three times do Justin and Trypho engage in a truly "Socratic" dialogue entailing a lively exchange, around the discussions concerning the scope of Jewish law and the birth of Christ from a virgin (Chapters 45–49, 67–68). Trypho's role can probably best be summarized in his own words, when he approaches Justin and requests, "Bring us on, then," said [Trypho], "by the Scriptures, that we may also be persuaded by you" (90:1).

Trypho's role is to learn from Justin the true interpretation of Scripture. For the most part, the form of the "dialogue" here is only an extremely thin veneer to what is, in truth, an ongoing lecture on biblical exegeses delivered by Justin.[9]

Not surprising, then, the teachings of the Jewish sages are cited by Justin rather than by Trypho, as we might have otherwise expected. Justin's goal is to drive a wedge between the educated, inquisitive Jews represented by Trypho, and the "sages" and leaders of the Jews. Justin says so almost explicitly, at the end of the work: "setting a higher value on the Christ of the Almighty God than on *your own teachers*" (142:2, emphasis mine). Note that, this sentence alone constitutes sufficient evidence against the attempt of some scholars to identify Trypho with the famous R. Tarfon.[10] As I have tried to show, Trypho is a pale character, unimpressive in his knowledge of Jewish teachings.

Much has been written about the correct, and even cordial, relations prevailing in the *Dialogue*.[11] Exceptional are Justin's virulent attacks against the Jewish teachers. The thrust of the attack is in the chapters where Trypho is silent (90–142). Following are several examples of Justin's slanderous attacks against Jewish teachers: "But if your teachers only expound to you why female camels are spoken of in this passage, and are not in that; or why so many measures of fine flour and so many measures of oil [are used] in the offerings; and do so in a low and sordid manner..." (112:4). The Jewish masters fail because they are "imprudent and blind" (134). Justin had already quoted (112) Jesus' judgment on the Jewish scribes—"You blind guides" (Matthew 23:24)—and here he appears only to be applying his master's teaching. The truth, however, is that Justin took it upon himself to disprove the exegetic method endorsed by Jewish sages and to persuade the Jews that no true interpretation of the Bible is possible without the grace of Jesus. In the final analysis, the Jews would have to choose between the exegeses of their inane teachers and those of the Master of the Universe's Messiah.

As for Justin's method in his exegetic contest with the Jews, it should be noted that the *Dialogue* is so confrontational that a true exchange is all but impossible. This contrasts sharply with the Church Fathers in the coming centuries, who will allow themselves to learn from Jewish exegeses, adopting some and rejecting others. The Christians will by then be sufficiently secure to allow cultivation of Jewish commentaries. In Justin's times, however, this was not the case. For Justin, the basic insensitivity of the Jewish teachers precluded any possibility of learning from their homilies. His main task was to persuade his public that the Jews' own scriptures had foretold the coming of Jesus and that, without this key, the true meaning of the Bible remained inaccessible. It is somewhat ironic that a work entitled *dialogue* belies any chance of shared study or genuine exchange between Christians and Jews.

Our discussion will revolve around two topics, central to the dialogue. The first is Justin's attack on Jewish observance of the commandments, including his explanations of why these laws were given to the Jews, and the relevance of these laws to the Christians of his time; the second is his exegesis of the biblical verses that he sees as heralding the coming of the Christ. After clarifying Justin's claims and methods, including those he ascribes to the Jewish teachers of his times, we will closely consider rabbinic midrashim of the same period, to estimate their relevance to the questions raised by Justin.

The preface to the section on the commandments appears immediately after the introductory chapters (1-9), where Justin describes his approach to philosophy and the revelation that brought him to Christianity. Trypho's reaction to Justin's story is that Justin would have done better if he had remained faithful to lofty philosophical values instead of placing his trust in a human being that is supposed to save him. The Jew Trypho goes on to offer his new friend even better advice: "If then, you are willing to listen to me (for I have already considered you a friend), first be circumcised, then observe what ordinances have been enacted with respect to the Sabbath, and the feasts, and the new moons of God; and, in a word, do all things which have been written in the law; and then perhaps you shall obtain mercy from God" (8:4). The Jew Trypho expands and sharpens his critique of Christianity in another chapter: "But this is what we are most at a loss about: that you professing to be pious, and supposing yourselves better than others, are not in any particular separated from them...in that you observe no festivals or sabbaths, and do not have the rite of circumcision; and further, resting your hopes on a man that was crucified, you yet expect to obtain some good thing from God, while you do not obey His commandments [*entolas*]" (10:3). In sum, Trypho is presented as seeking answers mainly to this last question—how can Christians hope for salvation without abiding by the Torah (*nomos*) (10:4).

In the next thirty chapters, Justin shows Trypho the real reasons for the commandments, and the commandments' true meaning in Christian perspective. Almost invariably, he relies on biblical verses and homilies for proof. Since the sabbath and circumcision are Trypho's foremost concern, Justin offers a variety of counterarguments, which can be grouped under three rubrics:[12]

1. From the Jewish sources themselves it appears that the commandments were not necessarily valid for all eternity. The true reason for giving these laws to the Jews was to rein in their obstinacy.
2. Neither nature nor God observe the commandments (for instance, the sabbath).
3. Christianity itself is the proper observance of the commandments. Christianity is a perpetual sabbath, not limited to one day of the week.

Justin attempts to undermine the foundation of the commandments by using what we may call the *bracket* argument. His main move is to show that, because according to the Torah, righteous people had existed prior to the giving of the commandments, it follows that there can be an era of "righteousness" that need not include observance of the Torah even after the giving of the commandments. Adam, Abel, Enoch, Noah, and Melchizedek symbolize "righteousness" in the precommandments era, while Christians do so in the postcommandments era. The covenant of the commandments is no longer valid and has been bracketed to a given time in history. All that Justin needs to do now is explain why it was necessary to give the commandments to the Jews in the first place. This is his reason: "that God enjoined you to keep the sabbath, and impose on you other precepts for a sign, as I have already said, on account of your unrighteousness [*adikias*] and that of your fathers…" (21:1). The signs of the covenant, the sabbath as well as circumcision, were seen by Justin as marks of disgrace, meant to warn the Jews and distance them from their evil ways. Instead of being understood as signs of chosenness, the commandments are to be perceived as punishments, meant to deter sinners. Were it not for the defiance and hard-heartedness of the Jews, the signs and commandments would have been unnecessary. The sin of the golden calf showed that Jews needed to offer sacrifices to God "in order that you might not serve idols" (19:6). The original, desirable state is that of those righteous people who lived without commandments. According to Justin, the commandments were given to the Jews only because they had failed. The prophets were forced to repeat and stress some of the commandments given by Moses, among them the sabbath, in the hope that this hard-hearted people [sklerokardion in Greek) would finally come back to its senses and repent.

Justin finds support in Ezekiel 20 for the view that the commandments were given as a punishment. He quotes from it at length, but without indicating how the text decisively supports his view. In this chapter, Ezekiel rebukes the people of Israel for their repeated perversions from the time of their sojourn in Egypt. We will quote the chapter from verse 5, though Justin begins with verse 20:

> and made myself known to them in the land of Egypt…then I said to them, Cast away every man the abomination of his eyes, and do not defile yourselves with the idols of Egypt.… But they rebelled against me, and would not hearken to me… then I said, I will pour out my fury upon them, to accomplish my anger against them in the midst of the land of Egypt. But I acted for my name's sake, that I should not be profaned in the sight of the nations.… And I caused them to go out of the land of Egypt, and brought them into the wilderness. And I gave them my statues, and made my judgments known to them, which if a man do, he may live by them. Moreover also I gave them my Sabbaths, to be a sign between me and them that they might know that I am the Lord who sanctify them… (Ezekiel 20:5–12)

Now we will quote the text that follows in Ezekiel, according to Justin's version, which is almost identical to that of the Septuagint:[13]

> I am the Lord your God; walk in my statutes, and keep My judgments and take no part in the customs of Egypt; and hallow My sabbaths, and they shall be a sign between Me and you that ye may know that I am the Lord your God. Notwithstanding ye rebelled against Me, and your children walked not in My statutes.... I lifted up Mine hand unto them in the wilderness, that I would scatter them among the heathen, and disperse them through the countries; because they had not executed My judgments, but had despised My statutes and polluted my sabbaths.... Wherefore I gave them also statutes that were not good, and judgments whereby they shall not live. And I shall pollute them in their own gifts... (21:2–4).

Is Justin's evidence in the phrase "statutes that were not good," taken to mean that God had given statutes because of the people who "were not good," because of those bad Jews? This might have been Justin's intention, but I believe that he is relying on the chapter as a whole, as might be suggested by his transposition of verse 7 ("take no part in the customs of Egypt") into the sequence of verses 20–26. Justin reads Ezekiel as follows: When Israel was chosen in Egypt, the people were told to refrain from defilement through Egyptian idols. The generation of Egypt failed, and the desert generation was given statutes and a sign and further warning against defilement. That generation failed too, however, until the last stage was reached—the destruction of the people, perhaps through bad statutes. The decline of the people, then, is the very reason for the statutes and the sign.

Justin's language is even more vitriolic when attacking circumcision. This sign attests to the fact that the Jews were truly not a people like all others, but a "no people," in the words of the prophet Hosea 1:9 (19:5). The sign is meant to single out the Jews—that only they should suffer the punishment they deserve because of their sins. And these are Justin's words:

For the circumcision according to the flesh, which is from Abraham, was given for a sign; that you may be separated from other nations, and from us; and that you alone may suffer that which you now justly suffer; and that your land may be desolate, and your cities burned with fire; and that strangers may eat your fruit in your presence, and not one of you may go up to Jerusalem.... For none of you, I suppose, will venture to say that God neither did nor does foresee the events, which are future, nor foreordained his deserts for each one. Accordingly, these things have happened to you in fairness and justice, for you have slain the Just One...cursing in your synagogues those that believe on Christ.[14] (16:2–4)

The anguish of the persecuted Christian of the mid-second century emerges clearly in this passage, but it cannot dull the bitterness of Justin's theological formulation. Justin's answer to Trypho's amazement over the fact that Christians do not separate from others is sharp and clear: Jews are separate because they had failed. Only for Jews were such extreme measures required, to restrain them and punish them. Jesus' disciples and followers surely do not require this separation, neither as a deterrent nor as a punishment.

Justin's explanation of why the commandments were given to the Jews may also suggest why they were given at that particular time. Justin strengthens his claim by pointing out two additional facts: (1) There is no indication that either God or nature abide by the commandments. (2) Commandments have been rejected or abrogated even within Judaism, proving that the commandments are contingent rather than absolute, as the Jews present them. Let us see how Justin formulates these claims.

First, says Justin, we have no sign that the elements rest on the Sabbath; as nature remains unchanging, so should human beings (23:3). This claim is quite elegant, even if lacking a defined Christian imprint. Justin does not resort to verses in this case, as his proof is ostensibly empirical; and he seems to have taken this claim ready-made from pagan critics of Judaism. To the Jews, this claim will have appeared less persuasive because, as is widely known, nature was never ordered to rest on the Sabbath! (On the Sambatyon River, see later.)

More interesting is Justin's attempt to demonstrate that even God does not rest on the Sabbath: "Be not offended at, or reproach us with, the bodily uncircumcision with which God has created us; and think it not strange that we drink hot water on the sabbaths, since God directs the government of the universe on this day equally as on all others; and the priests, as on other days, so on this, are ordered to offer sacrifices" (29:3). The order of the sacrifices in the temple, as well as the order of Creation, attest that the sabbath is not different from other days. The argument from the sacrifices and from Creation are linked together, but differ in character. The argument from the sabbath sacrifices is meant to attenuate the Jewish assertion that the commandments are eternally valid by showing that the Jewish system of laws undergoes changes and transformations. Elsewhere, Justin will rely on the fact that the commandment of circumcision supersedes the sabbath as an additional instance of this flexibility (27:5).[15] Jewish sources do discuss at great length the terms under which commandments supersede one another. Conflicts and contradictions between the commandments prove, according to Justin, that God had no intention of legislating for all generations because, had He wanted, He certainly could have prevented this undesirable result.

The argument that God does not rest on the sabbath might surprise and even confound a Jewish listener. When ordered to observe the sabbath, Jews are reminded, "for in six days God made heaven and earth, and on the seventh day he rested, and was refreshed" (Exodus 31:17). Justin then attempts to show that God does not respect His sabbaths. Jews surely knew that God was not bound to abide by the commandments, but perhaps found the notion that Jews rested on the sabbath in remembrance of God's rest, though God no longer does so, slightly annoying.[16]

Justin tried to deny Jewish commandments their authority but stopped short of rejecting them altogether; those now with authority were the Christians, who abide by the new Torah (*kainos nomos*). In my view, the tone of this controversy conveys Justin's loathing for what is, in his view, the Jews' exaggerated trust in the observance of the commandments and their reward: "The new law requires you to keep perpetual sabbath, and you, because you are idle for one day, suppose you are pious, not discerning why this has been commanded you" (12:5). The Jew who observed the commandments had no reason to be proud of this fact or boast about it. Not only were the commandments given as punishments, or as a special remedy against the disease afflicting the Jews, but Jews were also to understand, according to Justin, that even when they did observe the commandments, this is not truly the fulfillment of God's will. The Jew moves from one commandment to another to do God's will, while the Christian is continually doing God's will.

Nowhere in the *Dialogue* do we find the Jew making a truly serious attempt to answer these charges. In the defense of his heritage, Trypho the Jew was silenced.

Let us now examine whether the arguments advanced by Justin resonate in the rabbinic literature of this period. Is there any concern with the topics raised by Justin in the *Dialogue*? Can we find in rabbinic literature any "answers" to Justin's questions?

The Ideological Contest: The Dialogue Between Jews and Gentiles in *Genesis Rabbah*

In the previous chapter we saw Justin in his controversy with Trypho marshalling arguments against sabbath observance. Trypho had no answers. In this chapter we examine rabbinic sources and their sensitivity to the problems raised by Justin. It must be clarified that we are not assuming the rabbis were acquainted with Justin's *Dialogue*. Our concern is to establish whether our own knowledge of Justin's arguments contributes to a more sensitive reading of Midrash. In other words, can we identify attempts in rabbinic literature to ward off arguments of the type we encountered in Justin's work? Let us peruse a section of Genesis Rabbah wholly devoted to the sabbath; the passage assumes the form of an open controversy.

Genesis Rabbah is the oldest of the amoraic midrashim,[1] and was apparently redacted in the fifth century. Chapter 11 is wholly devoted to the sabbath and expounds essentially one verse: "And God blessed the seventh day, and sanctified it" (Genesis 2:3). This chapter is based on earlier tannaitic homilies, which treat the combination "And God blessed...and sanctified." These homilies first appear in the tannaitic midrash *Mekhilta de-Rabbi Ishmael*. We will first sample and juxtapose parallel passages from these two midrashim, in an attempt to take a close look at the approach of *Genesis Rabbah* and its faithfulness to its original source, the *Mekhilta*.

Genesis Rabbah (11)	*Mekhilta* (*Bahodesh* 7)
"And God blessed the seventh day and hallowed it." R. Ishmael said: "He blessed it" with manna "and	"Wherefore the Lord blessed the Sabbath Day and hallowed It. "He blessed it" with manna and "hallowed it" with

hallowed it" with manna, for every day of the week there descended one *omer* but on the eve of the Sabbath two *omers*; "And He hallowed it" through manna, which did not descend on the Sabbath at all.

R. Nathan said: "He blessed it" with manna and "hallowed it" with a blessing. R. Isaac said: "He blessed it" with manna, "and hallowed it" by the verdict on the wood gatherer (Numbers 15:35).

manna. These are the words of R. Ishmael.

R. Akiva says: "He blessed it" with manna "and hallowed it" with a blessing. R. Isaac said: "He blessed it" with manna, "and hallowed it" by the verdict on the wood gatherer (Numbers 15:35).

As the comparison shows, the beginning of the section in *Genesis Rabbah* is very close to the original in the *Mekhilta*. Two prominent differences are, first, the changes in the names—R. Akiva in the *Mekhilta* becomes R. Nathan in *Genesis Rabbah*—and second, the explanation following R. Ishmael's words in *Genesis Rabbah*. The kernel of this added explanation appears elsewhere in the *Mekhilta* itself (Vayassa 2): "For every day there was but one *omer*; for the Sabbath there were two *omers*." Whether it was the redactor of *Genesis Rabbah* who attached it here or whether this explanation was already included in the text of the *Mekhilta* available to him, this addition belongs to the tannaitic layer and was not written by the redactor of *Genesis Rabbah*. As for the names, note that the version in *Genesis Rabbah* mentioning R. Nathan, one of the central figures in the school of R. Ishmael (*Debei R. Ishmael*) is very appropriate, and is certainly a plausible transposition. Although the rest of this section in *Genesis Rabbah* represents a more radical departure from the *Mekhilta* and also adds amoraic material, it is important to note that, from the beginning, it is well anchored in the tannaitic source of the first two centuries C.E.

Let us move on to the central story in *Genesis Rabbah*, describing a dialogue between R. Akiva and Tineius Rufus ("Turnusrufus") the wicked.[2] This story is set among five teachings ascribed to the *tannaim*, placed after the last homily in the series

"Blessed it with...," which we quoted previously. The last homily—
"He blessed it with tasty dishes"—is immediately followed by a
story about the special taste of the sabbath dishes that the Rabbi
prepared for the Roman emperor Antoninus. Following is the story
of R. Akiva and Tineius Rufus, which opens with a question by
Tineius Rufus "Why does this day [the sabbath] differ from other
days?"

> The wicked Tineius Rufus asked R. Akiva: "What is a day
> from other days?" "What is a man from other men?" he
> retorted. "What did I say to you and what did you say to
> me?" said he. "You said to me," he replied, "why does the
> Sabbath differ from other days," and I answered you, "Why
> does Rufus differ from other men." "Because the emperor
> desired to honor him," said he. "Then this day, too, the Holy
> One wished to honor." "How can you prove it to me?" "Let
> the river Sambatyon prove it, which carries stones the whole
> week but allows them to rest on the Sabbath." "You are
> drawing me away" [evading the question]. "Then let him
> who brings up the dead prove it, for every day [the dead]
> come up but not on the Sabbath." He went and made a test
> with his own father: every day he came up, but on the
> Sabbath he did not come up. After the Sabbath he brought
> him up. "Father," said he, "have you become a Jew since your
> death? Why did you come up during the whole week but not
> on the Sabbath?" Said he: "He who does not keep the Sabbath
> among you of his own free will must keep it here in spite of
> himself." "But what toil have you there?" he demanded. "The
> whole week we are tortured but on the Sabbath we rest."
> Then he went back to R. Akiva and said to him: "If, as you
> say, the Holy One, blessed be He, honors the Sabbath, then let
> Him not stir up winds or cause the rain to fall on that day."
> "May the spirit depart such a man!" he exclaimed; He (God)
> is like one who carries four cubits."[3]

In sum, the story tells us that an important pagan told a leading
Jewish sage a riddle and received an answer in kind—another
riddle. The solution to both riddles is the same. A certain day and a

certain person become unique because the king wishes to honor them. The Jewish sage adduces supporting evidence from the natural and the supernatural realms, indicating that God honors the sabbath. The evidence from nature, a "sabbath-observing" river, is not acceptable to the pagan, who rejects it as implausible and evasive ("You are drawing me away"). The pagan's dead father is then brought in to confirm the testimony of the Jewish sage, who had argued that supernatural forces do observe the sabbath. The pagan then delivers his coup de grace: God, the Supreme Power, does not refrain from activating nature during the sabbath. God Himself, then, does not rest on the sabbath, does not "honor the sabbath." The Jew's answer is that the work performed by God during the sabbath is well within the range of labor halakha allows on this day.

This summary, however, leaves the interesting questions raised by this story unanswered. What is the meaning of the amusing dialogue between Tineius Rufus and his father? How serious is R. Akiva's last reply? Does he really believe that God "observes the sabbath" or is he simply dismissing the pagan with idle speculations? To what extent is this story paradigmatic of the dialogue between Jews and Gentiles at this time? Last, we will consider to what extent the "pagan's" arguments overlap those of Justin in the *Dialogue*.

Let us begin with the question of language. Note that R. Akiva's speech is reported in Rabbinic Hebrew rather than Aramaic. This is not a trivial issue, since *Genesis Rabbah* is an amoraic collection, presuming here to have preserved a conversation that took place in the first decades of the second century, during the tannaitic period. Was the midrash careful to preserve the language of the conversation as it could have been reported in the tannaitic literature of R. Akiva's times? The fact that almost all of R. Akiva's speech is delivered in Hebrew, except for the curse at the end ("May the spirit depart such a man!") helps to establish the credentials of this text as essentially tannaitic. The issue of "brings up the dead"[4] is also made clear in light of another tannaitic source (*Tosefta* Sanhedrin 10:7): "'A necromancer' (Deuteronomy 18:11) this is one who brings up the dead 'by witchcraft' (heb.-maaleh bezechuro).... What is the difference between one who brings up the dead by 'witchcraft' and one who asks a skull? That for one who brings up the dead by 'witchcraft,' [the dead] does not come up in the usual manner and does not come up on the Sabbath." On the other hand, Tineius Rufus' dialogue alternates between Hebrew and Aramaic. The language of the source, then, is inconclusive as to whether it reflects a tannaitic account of a conversation that, if it did take place, was probably conducted through a translator or in Greek!

Let us consider the structure of the story and its main characters.[5] The frame of the story is the exchange between Tineius Rufus and R. Akiva; at the beginning are the Roman's five questions and the Jew's five answers, and at the end, a question and answer. R. Akiva's two proofs are known from sources that predate *Genesis Rabbah*. The *Tosefta* had already stated that, on the sabbath, a particular form of witchcraft cannot be used to bring up the dead. The tradition about the river that stops its flow on the sabbath is already mentioned by Pliny the Elder in his first century tract, *Natural History*.[6] We could say that Tineius Rufus' main question concerns this world. The proof from the world of the dead is certainly impressive, and we will still return to it, but the concentrated thrust of the Roman's attack is directed against the fact that God does not cause nature to rest on the sabbath. R. Akiva's attempt to rely at first on proof from the River Sambatyon is rightfully rejected by the Roman as an oddity, if not a mere legend. R. Akiva's final answer invites different readings, to which we now turn.

It must be noted that the wording of the last sentence, although reasonably clear, is not totally smooth. Halakha forbids carrying objects in public on the sabbath four cubits [*dalet amot*] (about two meters).[7] Hence, we could have expected this midrash to read "one who carries *within* four cubits." The import of this sentence is reasonably clear, but we have found another version of *Genesis Rabbah* (Vatican Mss. 60),[8] where the wording is quite different, but the meaning is similar: "if only one lodger dwelt in the courtyard, he carries in the whole courtyard. So the Holy One, blessed be He, as the world and the fullness thereof is His, He carries in His whole world." The intention is the same in both versions: The Holy one observes the sabbath *according to the halakha*, and no transgression of the sabbath laws is entailed by the actions of nature. R. Akiva's "clincher" in our version is that the Holy one honors the sabbath exactly in line with the rulings of the Oral Law He gave to Israel. The actions of nature do not, in any way, contradict the sabbath commandments. This is not the only reply given in this section of *Genesis Rabbah* to the pagan claim, later adopted by Christians, that nature shows the commandments to be invalid.[9] In the next story, where R. Hoshaya speaks with "a philosopher" about circumcision, R. Hoshaya will argue that "whatever was created in the six days of Creation requires further preparation." Nature, then, needs to be completed, and it is shown that *natural* is not necessarily synonymous with *perfect*. I return to this claim later.

The most surprising passage in our story is certainly the conversation between Tineius Rufus and his father. We learn that his father is tortured [*nidonin*][10] the whole week, and rests on the sabbath. The answer to Tineius Rufus' amusing, ironic query—"Have you become a Jew since your death?"—is, conceptually, the surprise element in the story: "He who does not keep the sabbath among you of his own free will must keep it here in spite of himself." No option is offered in the next world, where *gentiles* who had refused to observe the sabbath in this one are now forced to do so. In fact, the advice of Tineius Rufus' father to him is that he should begin observing the sabbath laws. Is this some general prescription, as if the father were retorting in kind—"*You* become a Jew while you are still alive"—or is this the narrator calling on gentiles to observe the sabbath? Of these two options, the second seems actually more daring. It is well known that one view in rabbinic literature ruled out this possibility altogether—"A gentile who observes the sabbath deserves death" (Sanhedrin 58b).[11] On the other hand, it is quite clear that there were God-fearing gentiles, who did observe certain commandments. I am still inclined to endorse the more moderate interpretation, that this is a father pleading with his son to become a Jew.

As we follow the narrative unfolding, we see that Tineius Rufus is not persuaded by his father's appeal. He could simply have claimed that he now has proof that the supernatural world has place for sabbath observance, but the contradiction between halakha and nature still prevails. R. Akiva's answer to this objection, as we saw, is that the Holy one, blessed be He, activates nature without transgressing halakha. God, as it were, also observes the sabbath.

Before drawing conclusions from this source and comparing it with the claims advanced by Justin Martyr, we will do well to consider the next two sources in this section of *Genesis Rabbah* and then evaluate all three.

The link of the next story to the one on R. Akiva is that both describe disputes with a non-Jew regarding observance of the commandments. As noted, the controversy this time surfaces in a conversation about circumcision between R. Hoshaya and a philosopher. It must be noted that, in the whole chapter, this is the only source that is *not* concerned with the sabbath (except, perhaps, for a story on the Day of Atonement). It seems we can safely assume that the dialogue between R. Akiva and Tineius Rufus and the conversation between R. Hoshaya and the philosopher make up one polemical unit, dating from the end of the tannaitic and the beginning of the amoraic period.[12] We will elaborate on this point after expounding the second dialogue, in *Genesis Rabbah* 11:6:

> A philosopher asked R. Hoshaya: "If circumcision is precious, why was it not given to Adam? "If so," he replied, "why do you shave the corners of your head and leave your beard? "Because it grew with me wildly" was the answer. "If so, you should blind your eye and cut off your hands?" Said he: "To such an argument have we come!" "I cannot send you away empty-handed, (*halaq*)" said he. "[The real reason is this:]; whatever was created in the first six days required further preparation, e.g., mustard needs sweetening, vetch need sweetening, wheat needs grinding, and man too needs further correction."

Let us begin again with the linguistic aspect. The whole dialogue is conducted in Hebrew, except for the philosopher's expression of amazement. Who is this philosopher, R. Hoshaya's contemporary? Many scholars have attempted to identify him with Origen, the Church father who lived in Caesarea at the time and well deserved to be called a philosopher. The physical description of the philosopher cannot be considered decisive proof, since philosophers generally tended to grow wild beards. The word *given* used in regard to circumcision creates associations with "giving a commandment," bringing us closer to the question that could have been asked by a Christian. Nevertheless, this is not a specifically Christian exchange, and the answer to the Christian argument differs from the kind of reply we encountered, for instance, in Justin's *Dialogue*. The point here seems to be the question of why was not man created circumcised to begin with. Why is he not a finished product, like the rest of Creation? Indeed, in a parallel version found in *Pesikta Rabbati*, two stories were added following this dialogue, where the question is asked, "If circumcision is so beloved to the Holy one, blessed be He, why was its performance not included among the Ten Commandments?" As noted, timing is a very significant issue for Christianity.[13] In *Genesis Rabbah*, however, the question is not concerned with the issue of timing; rather it asks why was circumcision not included in the blueprint of Creation, part of human nature from the beginning? In fact, the biblical text almost begs this question, which could have been asked, just as well, by a Jew as by a non-Jew. It is fascinating to note that elsewhere in *Genesis Rabbah* (Chapter 46), this very question is ascribed to Abraham, who wants to know why, indeed, this "dear" commandment was not given to Adam!

R. Hoshaya tries a smart answer first, telling the philosopher that he himself has arbitrarily chosen to change the natural status of one part of his body ("shave the corners of his head") while leaving others alone. Rightfully, the philosopher replies that something growing wild differs from a human organ, and ridicules R. Hoshaya's answer—"To such an argument have we come?" Finally, R. Hoshaya deigns to answer more "seriously," although a jesting ring can still be detected here. The expression *lehotsyiaḥa ḥalak* [literally, "get you off smoothly"] to mean "send you away empty-handed" is quite rare[14] and seems to suggest a play of words on the topic of hair that opened the conversation (hairy-smooth, see Jacob's story in Genesis 27:11). At all events, his answer is that nature needs finishing, and so does the physical nature of human beings.

As an interim summary, we will suggest that the two conversations we have just discussed touch on the problem of the relation between the commandments and nature. The first conversation claims that the actions of nature are bound by the sabbath laws and the second claims that nature is not necessarily perfect and may require "amendment." The commandments are thus intended to amend and complete nature. These two conversations, together with the two previous ones—that between R. Judah Hanasi and Antoninus, and the question R. Ishmael b. R. Yose asks of R. Judah Hanasi—make up a unit, where the main speakers are *tannaim* and the first generation of *amoraim*. Another tannaitic source, the last in the series, closes this unit. *Genesis Rabbah* will then return to the standard exegetic framework and, following the first question in this section—"Wherewith did he bless it?"—will turn to the second—"Why did He bless it?" Our concern is, precisely, the series of dialogues, mainly ascribed to the *tannaim*, interpolated between the unit "Wherewith did he bless it?" and the unit "Why did he bless it?" The series does not end with a dialogue but with a conventional, even if slightly odd homily. Let us consider it in more detail before attempting to draw conclusions about this middle section as a whole, as well as its associations with similar claims raised by both Christians and pagans.

The homily is cited by R. Yohanan in the name of R. Yose. Some of the parallel versions (for instance, *Pesikta Rabbati*) explicitly mention R. Yose b. Halafta, the *tanna* who was R. Akiva's disciple:

> Abraham, who is not reported to have kept the Sabbath, inherited the world in [limited] measure, as it is written, "arise, walk through the land in the length of it and in the breadth of it [Genesis 13:17). But Jacob, of whom the keeping of the Sabbath is mentioned—"And he encamped before the city (Genesis 33:18)—entered at twilight and set boundaries before sunset, and inherited the world without measure— "And thou shalt spread abroad to the west, and to the east..." Genesis 28:14).

It must be noted that this homily does not explicitly say that Abraham did not observe the sabbath, but that his sabbath observance was not reported in Scripture.[15] A well-known homily claims that Abraham did abide by all the commandments of the Torah, even before it was given.[16] Indeed, R. Yose could well be understood as claiming here that Abraham did not keep the sabbath, but the language of the homily nevertheless supports the view that the intention of this homily is that Abraham's observance of the sabbath did not merit as much attention as Jacob's. (The fact that this homily relies on yet another one—"And he encamped before the city," meaning he set boundaries before the Sabbath—is standard for the Aggada). What matters is that R. Yose wanted to minimize Abraham's sabbath observance vis-à-vis that of his grandson. Jacob inherited a boundless land because he set limits before the sabbath. Abraham did not receive a full inheritance because he did not excel as a sabbath observer.

One of the main motivations behind this homily is certainly the attempt to emphasize the notion that sabbath observance was important for inheriting the land. This is not a surprising statement from the mouth of a sage living after Bar Kokhba's rebellion, who tried to encourage sabbath observance by suggesting to the people it could help them regain the legacy they had lost in the war. The idea and the possible motivation are clear, but why comfort the people at Abraham's expense?

R. Yose's words could also be seen as contesting a view we encountered in the *Dialogue*. According to this view, which is anchored in Paul, Abraham is perfect merely by virtue of his faith and had no need for the commandments. R. Yose wishes to argue that this is not so. Even Abraham did not receive his full inheritance because he was not explicitly mentioned as a sabbath observer, and only he who endeavors to observe the sabbath will inherit a boundless land.

To clarify our conclusions from this tannaitic anthology preserved in *Genesis Rabbah*, we present a summary of the discussion so far, including the structure of the series and the homilies preceding it and following it: "He blessed it with tasty dishes"

1. The Sabbath meal prepared by R. Judah Hanasi for Antoninus (a unique spice called *sabbath*). The cold sabbath dishes are tastier than the hot food of all other days.
2. R. Ishmael b. R. Yose learns from R. Judah Hanasi that the people of the Diaspora live long lives because they honor the sabbath.

(Two amoraic stories on honoring the sabbath and the Day of Atonement follow)

3. Tineius Rufus and R. Akiva.
4. A philosopher and R. Hoshaya.
5. R. Yohanan in the name of R. Yose—on the sabbath observance of Abraham and Jacob.
   "And why did He bless it"…

This series raises the following points regarding the sabbath: sabbath dishes taste different—a kind of natural uniqueness informs the sabbath, which is also recognizable by a non-Jew (1); the reward of sabbath observance is long life for those who live in the Diaspora (2); the uninterrupted activity of nature does not refute the claim that the Holy One, blessed be He, keeps the sabbath (3); what is natural, is not necessarily perfect (4); the reward of the sabbath is a boundless inheritance (5).

In addition to the contents, it must be stressed that the three conversations of the sages with two emperors and a philosopher (1, 3, 4) were meant to refute evidence regarding the activity of nature on the sabbath (1, 3) and regarding the relationship between halakha and nature (3, 4). The sages' partners to these dialogues are not portrayed as heretics or Christians but as pagans who show an interest in, or challenge, Judaism. For these reasons, I believe this is not a dispute with Christians but part of an older controversy with pagans. Justin successfully integrated some of these arguments in his own work, as they would seem plausible to pagans and might even draw them to Christianity. The Jewish reactions do not resonate at all in Justin's work, although Jews certainly tried to reconcile the relation between nature and Torah. It is hard to decide whether Justin deliberately overlooked such Jewish attempts or he was simply unaware of them. Nevertheless, I believe that we can learn from this series of homilies about a controversy within rabbinic literature.

Three dialogues between gentiles and Jewish sages were assembled together, unified thematically, with one exception. Does this perhaps point to the existence of a literary genre in the model of conversations between gentiles and Jews, on which the redactor drew? If the answer to this question is yes, this might support the claim of historians who believed that pagans and Jews were indeed engaged in a dialogue at the time. Justin, who, according to the latest studies was well versed in the philosophy of his time, built his case on arguments against Judaism routinely voiced by pagans in the Greco-Roman world and incorporated them in his own attack against Judaism.

6

The *Dialogue with Trypho* and the *Mekhilta*: Selected Comparisons

In this chapter, we compare the approach to two themes in Justin's tract and in the *Mekhilta de-Rabbi Ishmael*. The *Mekhilta* is a *midrash halakha* on selected topics in the book of Exodus, edited close to the end of the tannaitic period, around the middle of the third century.[1] In addition to halakhic homilies, this midrash includes abundant aggadic material. Whereas in the previous chapter we endeavored to prove that the amoraic midrash *Genesis Rabbah* preserved tannaitic sources, the homilies in the *Mekhilta* are definitely held to be tannaitic, dating back to Justin's times and, in some cases, even before. We open with a definition of Judaism suggested by Justin, and contrast it with a similar "definition" in the *Mekhilta*. We will then consider the homiletic approaches adopted in these two works.

In Chapter 46 of the *Dialogue*, Trypho asks Justin the following question: What is the fate of a Jew who has been persuaded of the truth of Christianity but continues to observe the commandments? Will he also be saved? After a brief discussion, Justin claims that such a Jew will, indeed, be saved, as long as he does not attempt to persuade gentile Christians to abide by Jewish law in addition to their Christian faith (47:1). At the beginning of this discussion, Justin again asks the Jew for a list of the commandments that can still be observed after the destruction of the Temple. Trypho's answer is extremely interesting: "To keep the Sabbath, to be circumcised, to observe months, and to be washed if you touch anything prohibited by Moses, or after sexual intercourse" (46:2). Nations living in the Greco-Roman world saw the sabbath and circumcision as the quintessential signs of Judaism,[2] and it is self-evident why these two commandments were included in this list.

Not so the next two items in Trypho's short list. What does it mean "to observe months"? Was immersion still important after the destruction of the Temple? On the other hand, we could certainly expect that laws regarding forbidden foods and *kashrut* would find their place in a short list of commandments in force after the destruction of the Temple. If Trypho was indeed one of a group of Palestinian sages, he would certainly have included the study of Torah in this list. Trypho's list is surprising, because of what it contains as much as because of what it omits.

What were Justin's sources when he drew up this list on the principles of Judaism and made Trypho its spokesman? And if such a dialogue did take place between a Jew and Justin, on what did the Jew rely when formulating his thumbnail definition? First, the importance ascribed to "the month" is more suited to the biblical than to the tannaitic period; indeed, it seems to me that Justin relied here mainly on Isaiah's ideas—"as for new moons and sabbaths and the calling of assemblies" (1:13); "Also the sons of the stranger, that join themselves to the Lord to serve Him, to be his servants every one that keeps the sabbath and does not profane it, and all that take hold of my covenant" (56:6); "And it shall come to pass, that every new moon, and every sabbath, shall all flesh come to bow down to the ground before me" (66:23). The crux of Trypho's list appears to draw on Isaiah's theology, although not firsthand. Instead, it appears to be mediated by several controversial passages in the New Testament. Take, for instance, the Epistle to the Colossians (2:16) "Let no man therefore judge you in meat, or in drink, or in respect of any holiday, or of the new moon, or of the sabbath days." In adding "month" to this list, Trypho could be taking into account the fact that the Jewish patriarch ascribed special importance to the fixing of the month (see, for instance, *M. Rosh Hashanah* 2:9). However, the influence of Isaiah on Justin's work, filtered through what was to become the New Testament, appears to be stronger than the concern with the authority of the *nasi* of the Sanhedrin who, as far as I know, is never mentioned in this work.

We must still clarify the special role of immersion in Trypho's list, and two explanations seem possible. Justin may have wished immersion to be considered the main commandment since he himself, in previous chapters, had tried to demonstrate the significance of the Christian baptism:[3] "And we have received it [circumcision] through baptism, since we were sinners, by God's mercy; and all men may equally obtain it" (43:2). On the other hand, this may truly reflect the Jewish order of priorities in Justin's times.[4] A special passage in the *Mekhilta* deserves our attention in this context. The homilies expound verses 16–17 in Exodus 31: "Wherefore the children of Israel shall keep the Sabbath…. It is a sign between me and the children of Israel for ever…":

> "Between Me and the children of Israel." But not between Me and the nations of the world. "It is a sign for ever." This tells that the Sabbath will never be abolished from Israel. And so you find that all things for which Israel have laid down their lives have been preserved among them. And things for which Israel have not laid down their lives have not been retained by them. Thus the Sabbath, circumcision, the study of Torah, and the ritual of immersion, for which they laid down their lives, have been retained by them. But the Temple, civil courts, and the sabbatical and jubilee years, for which Israel did not lay down their lives, have not been preserved among them. (*Mekhilta, Shabbta* Ch. 1)

The homilies opening this passage are merely the negative conclusions drawn from the biblical verse—what Scripture asserts in a positive formulation, the midrash uses to draw a negative inference. However, the language of the midrash is highly polemic. It stresses the uniqueness of Israel and its eternal link with the sabbath. The sabbath was not given for a limited period, but forever. Did the homilist wish to enter here into a polemic with Christian arguments of the kind suggested by Justin? Because the homily adheres closely to the literal meaning of the verse, I would hesitate to answer this question with an unequivocal yes, although I am inclined to think so. The rest of the homily helps to support the view of this passage as a reaction to Christian claims.

The sabbath, circumcision, and the study of Torah are certainly three things for which Israel were willing to die, especially if we explain the expression *nat'nu et nafshan* as sacrificed their souls;[5] namely, they died for these commandments. Where is "immersion" in this list? Let us consider, for instance, the famous passage expounding three words in the Ten Commandments (*Mekhilta, Bahodesh*, Ch. 6 Lauterbach ed. p. 247):

> R. Nathan says: "Of them that love Me and keep My commandments," refers to those who dwell in the land of Israel and lay down their lives [*not'nin et nafsham*] for the sake of the commandments.[6] "Why are you being led out to be decapitated?" "Because I circumcised my son." "Why are you being led out to be burned?" "Because I read the Torah." "Why are you being led out to be crucified?" "Because I ate the unleavened bread." "Why are you getting a hundred lashes?" "Because I performed the ceremony of *lulav*"...

This source is useful on two counts. It uses the expression *not'nin et nafshan* to denote, unequivocally, the notion of "dying for." Second, when R. Nathan lists the commandments that Israel gave their lives for, he does not include immersion. Indeed, I have not found another instance of this use of immersion in the entire corpus of tannaitic literature.

I do not mean to diminish the importance of purity rituals. It is known that, according to one source, "purity spread in Israel" during the time of the Second Temple.[7] Even after the destruction of the Temple, several sages, who were not priests, took upon themselves to observe the purity rituals regarding food originally incumbent only on priests. Can the polemical tone adopted by the *Mekhilta* on the issue of the sabbath, as we saw, explain the appearance of immersion in a list of practices for which the people of Israel laid down their lives? It is as if to say, ritual immersion always had a central place, to the point that Jews were just as willing to lay down their lives for it as they were for the well-known commandments of sabbath, circumcision, and the study of Torah. This is not a unique feature of the new religion.

If we reject this option and uphold the view that the emphasis on ritual immersion in the *Mekhilta* is not guided by polemical considerations but reflects a basic, deep-rooted belief, then the list of items mentioned by Trypho overlaps the fundamental elements of the Torah presented in the *Mekhilta*, except for Justin's omission of Torah study. Hence, I believe that the comparison with the *Mekhilta* lends credence to Trypho's list in the *Dialogue* (46). The two issues omitted from the list—Torah study and abstention from certain foods—are not analogous. Justin had already dealt with the abstention from certain foods in Chapter 20, dismissing it as yet another law given to the Jews because of their inclination to forget God. In contrast, the commandment to teach Torah, which is certainly fundamental to the rabbinic approach, is not mentioned at all in the *Dialogue*. Again, this may reflect quite accurately the approach of a Palestinian Jew who was not one of the sages, or even one of their disciples. As mentioned in Chapter 4, most of the information regarding Jewish practices and exegeses is delivered by Justin, who mentions it in order to refute it. The "Jew" Trypho knows very little about the Jewish traditions he transmits in this work. Quite plausibly, then, a Jew like Trypho will not include the study of Torah among the commandments used to identify an average Jew.

We have so far seen Justin's attempt to undermine the essential elements of observance. In the section of the book discussing the commandments (10–47), he often quotes the prophets who chastised Israel in their time, as proof of his thesis that the commandments were given to restrain a profligate people. Nevertheless, this section also includes several examples of typological interpretations of these same commandments, where Justin presumes to disclose the true intention of Scripture. In the typological approach, every biblical statement is interpreted as a "type," as a symbol of the referent it represents. In Chapters 40–47 Justin shows, for instance, that the sacrifice of Passover and the Day of Atonement [*Yom Kippur*] are only symbols of Jesus, and circumcision on the eighth day alludes to the true circumcision, the resurrection of Jesus on the eighth day, Sunday.

Justin also uses the typological approach in the chapters intent on establishing that Jesus is the Messiah (48–108). These chapters contain several typological homilies that have parallels in the *Mekhilta*. This comparison will enable us to highlight the exegetical and homiletical approaches endorsed by both religions. In attempting to prove that Jesus is the Messiah, Justin's chief strategy is to show that prophecies and biblical verses are best understood when seen as predictions about the coming of Jesus.[8] The details of the life, death, and resurrection of Jesus supply the true key to the understanding of the Bible. For instance, Justin claims that the Psalms, which Jews interpreted as speaking of the House of David—of David himself, his son Solomon, or King Hezekiah—can be fully understood only when viewed as dealing with that special and unique descendant of the House of David— Jesus Christ.

Justin's strategy will be described in relation to three passages that are also discussed in the *Mekhilta.* Trypho finds it hard to understand why Jesus had to suffer such a disgraceful and humiliating death if he was indeed the Messiah. Trypho adds a request to this question: "Bring us on, then, said [Trypho], "by the Scriptures, that we may also be persuaded by you" (90:1). Surely this is Justin's belief, which he placed here in the mouth of the Jew. Justin believes that his exegesis of Scripture can convince the Jews of the justice of his claims, and dissuade them from listening to the inane interpretations of their own sages. Before answering Trypho's request, Justin alludes to an hermeneutic principle on which both of them have already agreed: "that what the prophets said and did they veiled by parables and types, as you admitted to us; so that it was not easy for all to understand the most [of what they said]..." (90:2). Justin now turns to the biblical verses he uses as his "raw material," showing that each story is a symbol of Jesus' life and even explicitly intimates the importance of the cross. The first story in the series is about the war with Amalek: Joshua fought with Amalek, while Moses climbed the hill, "And it came to pass, when Moses held up his hand, that Israel prevailed...and Aaron and Hur supported his hands; the one on the one side, and the other on the other side" (Exodus 17:11–12). Justin expounds Moses' actions as follows: "For it was not because Moses so prayed that the people were stronger, but because, while one who bore the name of Jesus [Joshua] was in the forefront of the battle, he himself [Moses] made the sign of the cross" (90:5). The combination of Jesus' name and the sign of the cross is what saved Israel from Amalek.

This lesson in the "authentic" exegesis of Scripture is interrupted for the next two chapters to allow Justin to return to the subject of the Jews' bad temper, which had forced God to give them the commandments. Because the Jews have no love for God and no love for their fellow beings, they curse the believers in Jesus and refuse to understand correctly the unmistakable signs given in the Torah (92–93). This protracted slander prepares the ground for the continuation of the lesson in typological exegesis, which this time focuses on the brass serpent (Numbers 21:4–10). Is it possible, asks Justin, that the same God who forbids idols and images would order Moses to make a brass serpent to heal the people? Justin has a ready answer: "He proclaimed the mystery, by which He declared that He would break the power of the serpent which occasioned the transgression of Adam, and [would bring] to them that believe in Him [who was foreshadowed] by this sign, i.e., Him who was to be crucified, salvation from the fangs of the serpent…" (94:2).[9] Justin is not satisfied with suggesting his own exegesis and continues his attack by inquiring how else Moses' acts can be described. This strongly worded question moves one of the Jews listening to the conversation to "confess": "For I have frequently interrogated the teachers about this matter, and none of them gave me a reason" (94:4), thus confirming Justin's persistent claim that he, and not the Jewish sages, holds the key to the true interpretation of the Scriptures.

After these two examples, Justin devotes several chapters to explain Psalms 22:2, "My God, my God, why has thou forsaken me?" He summarizes his approach in Chapter 111, where he adds two homilies on the healing powers of the blood of the Passover and of the scarlet thread in the story of Rahab, which symbolize the salvation attained through the blood of Jesus. This is what he writes on the blood of the Passover: "Would God then have been deceived if this sign had not been above the doors? I do not say that; but I affirm that He announced beforehand the future salvation for the human race through the blood of Christ." According to his translators, Justin uses the word sign here (semeia) in the sense of "cross"—in other words, the blood on the lintel and the sides of the doors created the shape of a cross.[10] If this translation is correct, then this is the third homily on the power of the cross and its symbol in Scripture. I am not convinced, however, that Justin is not referring here to the power of the blood rather than to the cross, as he expounds later concerning the Rahab story.

Justin concludes the presentation of his homiletical method with a brutal attack against the exegetic approach of the sages (Chapters 112–114), who ascribe failings to God, do not understand the symbolic nature of Scripture, and even believe that God has hands and feet and was revealed to the forefathers (114:3). As we saw in the previous chapter, Trypho has no answer to the accusations Justin hurls at the Jewish sages. It is interesting to note that some contemporary scholars tend to accept Justin's claims regarding the Jewish perception of God.[11] In any event, Jews were no doubt aware of the problematic verses cited by Justin and expounded them in their own way. Let us now consider the section of the *Mekhilta* where the three issues we have considered so far—the war with Amalek, the brass serpent, and the blood of the Passover—are grouped together:

We read in the *Mekhilta, Amalek* Ch. 1 (Lauterbach ed., p. 143–144):[12] "'And it came to pass, when Moses held up his hand'—Now, could Moses' hands make Israel victorious, or could his hands break Amalek? It means this: When Moses raised his hands toward heaven, the Israelites would look at him and believe in Him who had commanded Moses to do so; then God would perform for them miracles and mighty deeds." The *Mekhilta* denies any magic or symbolic power to Moses' act. Holding up his hands was an act intended to direct the children of Israel to believe in Him who ordered Moses to behave in this manner. Further on we read: "Similar to this: 'And God said to Moses: "Make thee a fiery serpent..."' Now, could that serpent kill or make alive? It means this: When Moses did so, the Israelites would look at him and believe in Him who had commanded Moses to do so; then God would send them healing." The same two passages that Justin considered conclusive support for his view that only symbolic interpretations are possible are also discussed together in the *Mekhilta*, but without transgressing the literal meaning. On the contrary: the rabbis present both the serpent and Moses as instruments, charged with directing our attention toward Moses' compliance with God's commandments and to rekindle Israel's faith in God.

As for the form, we see that both homilies in the *Mekhilta* begin from and return to the same point, using parallel linguistic forms. The question is, Now, do Moses' hands or the serpent have the power to generate miracles? The answer is that the healing and saving power is the power of faith in God, in "Him who commanded," in the God of the commandments. Is this midrash a response, a reaction, to Justin's? Or did Justin know homilies of the type we have found in the *Mekhilta* and sought to answer with a homily of his own, which would emphasize the principles of his religion? Before we answer these questions, let us consider two other homilies appearing in the *Mekhilta* immediately after. One concludes the two we have just seen whereas the other, a fascinating commentary, stands alone: "Similar to this: 'And the blood shall be to you for a token...' (Ex. 12:13). Now, of what use could the blood be to the angel or help the Israelites? It means this: When the Israelites did so and put some blood upon their doors, the Holy One, blessed be He, had pity on them, as it is said, 'The Lord will pass over...'" A slightly different pattern emerges here, since there is no specific stress on faith in "Him who commanded," but on action—Israel put blood on their doors. We could say that this very action proclaims their faith in Him who commanded them to do this. In and of itself, however, blood has no power and is only a concrete expression of their faith.[13]

What motivated the redactor of the *Mekhilta*, or of this sub-collection of "similar to this" homilies, to assemble these three examples together in one unit?[14] One obvious common denominator is that the three ostensibly describe magic activities proper, meant to coerce the higher power to abide by the magician's wishes. The answer of the midrash is—quite the contrary, God Himself commanded this behavior and the power of this act rests on its compliance with an order rather than on the act itself. This is neither magic nor theurgy, but a divine command. I believe we can safely assume there is a polemic here or an ideological struggle against pagan perceptions of this act as mere magic.[15] Very possibly, however, laying stress on faith in He who *commanded* is meant to divert this Jewish polemic and turn it against Christians.

Justin sought to channel these "hard" issues into a more "traditional" course. He added one important argument: these issues contradict other biblical stories that cannot possibly be interpreted "literally." These stories are meant only to symbolize the power of the Messiah, who is identified with the cross and with the name of Joshua.

We have so far seen a considerable difference between Justin's and the rabbinic approaches to these issues. Our reading of the *Mekhilta* is not yet finished. The last view cited in the *Mekhilta* is R. Eliezer's, who preceded Justin by a generation:[16] "For what purpose does it say 'Israel prevailed' or 'Amalek prevailed'? To tell that when Moses raised his hands toward heaven, it meant that Israel would be strong in the words of Torah, to be given through Moses' hands. And when he lowered his hands, it meant that Israel would lower their zeal for the words of Torah to be given through his hands." R. Eliezer explains that Moses' hands symbolize the words of Torah to be given by him, and holding up his hands means enhancing the study of Torah in the future. Is R. Eliezer's homily meant to uproot the literal meaning, or does it merely add another layer to it? I tend to endorse the latter option, thus drawing a clear distinction between him and Justin, who had meant to eradicate the literal layer altogether. This does not diminish the basic similarity between R. Eliezer's homiletic approach and that of Justin. Whereas for R. Eliezer the hands symbolize words of Torah, for Justin their shape symbolizes a cross.

Does our analysis of the war with Amalek, the brass serpent, and the blood of Passover in the *Mekhilta* and the *Dialogue* suggest any mutual dependence? It would not seem so. Each one of these works expounds these problematic verses in its own way, and we need not assume they knew of each other. Nevertheless, and despite the differences, a basic affinity prevails between R. Eliezer's and Justin's homilies, and the stress on the commanding God in the *Mekhilta* could suggest a polemic against Christianity.

I have emphasized the affinity between R. Eliezer and Justin to refute another of Justin's arguments. Justin accuses the sages of expounding Scripture in a low and sordid manner (112:4), and of listening to the words without investigating their force (112:1). He also claims that the Jewish sages believe that God has hands and feet (114:3). Because this work is concerned with the exegetic approaches of both religions, I will confine myself to these accusations and will not deal with more offensive slanders (see, for instance, 134:1). Justin was not thinking of a Jewish sage like Philo, who is surely an unsuitable target of such accusations; rather, his attack was intended against the exegetic approaches known to us from rabbinic literature. Justin points to several Jewish teachings, for which close parallels in rabbinic literature can be found.[17] His most impressive example is probably the three exegeses he ascribes to Jews of the verse "let us make man in our image," which are found in *Genesis Rabbah*. On the other hand, Justin's writings have preserved other exegeses that seem Jewish, but are not known to us from a Jewish source. One example is the homily where, according to Justin, Jews expound the verse "as the green herb" (Genesis 9:3): Just as we do not eat certain herbs, so from Noah's time we have been commanded [the same regarding certain animals] (20:2). We have found no trace of this homily. In fact, the opposite is true. Generally, this verse teaches us that Noah, unlike Adam, was allowed to eat of every animal.[18] Justin's knowledge of Jewish sources, however, is far from comprehensive. Quite clearly, most of what he cites in the name of the Jews revolves around biblical chapters that Christians saw as heralding Jesus, while Jews expounded them as relating to kings of the house of David.[19] Justin also relied on another source of information about Jews; namely, attitudes Jews had adopted against Christians and Christianity (not to speak to them, to curse them in the synagogue, to view Jesus as a sorcerer, and more).[20] Justin had some knowledge of Jewish society, for instance, that the sages allow Jews to marry four or five wives,[21] but his knowledge of Jewish exegesis in general and rabbinic exegesis in particular is, on the whole, unimpressive.

The rabbis also knew how to transcend the literal level when expounding Scripture, especially in their legends, not unlike Justin. What made rabbinic exegesis low and sordid in Justin's eyes is that the rabbis were blind to what, for him, was the only true interpretation of Scripture; namely, the one claiming that the Bible heralds Jesus Christ and the story of his life. Justin's work is an impressive attempt to wean away enlightened, Greek-speaking Jews from rabbinic interpretations and persuade them that the Christian exegesis is the only correct one. In his attempt to drive a wedge between the Jewish people and its sages, Justin mustered every possible slander against the rabbis, including the claim that the rabbis believed God has hands and feet.

Notwithstanding many exaggerations and overstatements in some of Justin's claims, we have tried to show that rabbinic literature is sensitive to the type of argument raised by Justin and his predecessors, both pagan and Christian. In the final analysis, Justin believed that he had obtained his interpretation of Scripture through an act of grace, through the revelation of the old man on the seashore depicted in the first chapters of the book. Not by chance, the book ends when Justin himself bids farewell to the Jews before setting sail and wishes them "to be earnest in setting a higher value of the Christ of the Almighty God than on your own teachers" (142:2). Even this literary convention may have a parallel in a long homily at the opening of the *Mekhilta*, where it is clarified that the land of Israel was chosen from among all others for the purpose of prophecy. Those who told their prophecies overseas were able to do so because of the merit of their own ancestors, and "He only spoke to them at a pure spot, near water."

7

Passover and the Exodus in Origen's Writings and Rabbinic Midrashim

Justin's zeal to persuade his interlocutor turns his work into a contentious polemic rather than a true dialogue. A spirit of confrontation thus clouds the words of Scripture, to their detriment. A very different picture emerges when considering Origen and his work, the subject of this chapter.

From his youth, Origen had endeavored to uncover the treasures of the Bible and throughout his life devoted himself to its study. One Origen scholar claims that "Origen was the first Christian father to devote himself fully to the study of the Bible."[1] Even Origen's foes within the Church, whose numbers increased significantly from the fourth century onward, conceded his encyclopedic knowledge of Scripture as well as his unique powers of interpretation. Together with his desire to find spiritual and even mystical meanings in Scripture, Origen was also attentive to detail and interested himself in the different versions of the biblical text. These concerns are reflected in his famous treatise, the *Hexapla*, made up of six parallel columns presenting versions of the Bible in Hebrew and in Greek.[2] This undertaking reflects his earnestness and his devotion to Scripture. His yearning to understand Scripture also led him to enter into arguments with Jews, and he often cites their exegeses as Jewish teachings, in a true scholarly spirit and without any polemical overtones.[3]

Origen was born in Alexandria, c. 185 C.E., to Christian parents who gave him a classical as well as a biblical education. His father died as a martyr in one of the persecutions Christians suffered under the Severan dynasty, and Origen himself apparently dies as a result of the persecutions of Decius, which began in 250 C.E. From 234 C.E. and until his death Origen lived in Caesarea, where he studied, preached, and wrote many books.[4] He had also been highly prolific in Alexandria, writing among other works, commentaries on the Bible and the New Testament. Our focus will be on his homiletic work in Caesarea, which according to Pierre Nautin, he produced from 239 or 240 onward.[5] Our aim is to outline the contents and the style of Origen's sermons dealing with the Exodus and Passover, compare them with rabbinic homilies on the same topics, and thereby acquire a special perspective on rabbinic Midrash.

Following is a review of the structure of Origen's homilies on the Book of Exodus, which includes thirteen sermons focusing on the following topics and chapters:

1.	Israel in Egypt	1:1–1:16
2.	On the midwives and the birth of Moses	1:15–2:10
3.	On feebleness in speech	4:10–5:24
4.	On the ten plagues	7:10–9:23
5.	On the departure of the children of Israel	12:37–14:30
6.	On Moses' and Miriam's song	15:1–15:19
7.	On the bitterness of water at Mara	15:23–16:14
8.	On the beginning of the Decalogue	20:2–20:6
9.	On the tabernacle	25:40
10.	On the miscarriage of a pregnant woman	21:22–21:25
11.	On the thirst in Rephidim, on the war with Amalek, and on the assistance of Jethro	17:3, 17:9, 18:21–22
12.	On the glorified countenance of Moses; the veil	34:30
13.	On the offerings for the tabernacle	35:4

As we can see, Origen covered the main topics in the book of Exodus in their proper order (except for around the tenth sermon).[6] Generally, his sermons open with a preface, move on to the main theme of the text and conclude with a doxology, that is, a formulaic rendering of the principles of faith. In Origen's work, the concluding phrase is, almost invariably, "to whom belongs glory [*doxa*], and sovereignty [*kratos*] forever and ever. Amen," taken from the First Letter of Peter (4:11). Following the sermon there was prayer and, at times, a "kiss of peace." During the sermon, the congregation sat before the bishop, who sat on a raised chair, and all the other priests sat before them in a semicircle.[7]

A more detailed analysis of the fifth sermon will help to clarify Origen's aims in his sermons in general, revealing something of their beauty. As we saw, like all skilled rhetors of his time, Origen opens with a brief preface. In the fifth sermon, the preface contains an important methodological declaration about the appropriate approach to the interpretation of Scripture:[8]

The Apostle Paul, "teacher of the Gentiles in faith and truth" (I Timothy 2:7) taught the Church which he gathered from the Gentiles how it ought to interpret the books of the Law...he gives some examples of interpretation that we might also note similar things in other passages, lest we believe that by imitation of the text and documents of the Jews we be made disciples. He wishes, therefore, to distinguish disciples of Christ from disciples of the Synagogue by the way they understand the Law. The Jews, by misunderstanding it, rejected Christ. We, by understanding the Law spiritually, show that it was justly given for the instruction of the Church. The Jews, therefore, understand only this, that "the children of Israel departed" from Egypt and their first departure was "from Ramesse" and they departed from there and came "to Socoth"... Then, next, they understand that there the cloud preceded them and the "rock" from which they drank water followed; and furthermore, they crossed the Read Sea and came into the desert of Sina. Let us see, however, what sort of rule of interpretation the Apostle Paul taught us about these matters. Writing to the Corinthians he says in a certain passage, "For we know that our fathers were all under the cloud, and all were baptized in Moses in the cloud and in the sea, and ate the same spiritual food and drank the same spiritual drink. And they drank of the spiritual rock which followed them, and the rock was Christ." (I Corinthians 10:1–4) Do you see how much Paul's teaching differs from the literal meaning? What the Jews supposed to be a crossing of the sea, Paul calls a baptism; what they supposed to be a cloud, Paul asserts is the Holy Spirit.... What then are we to do who received such instructions about interpretation from Paul, a teacher of the Church? Does it not seem right that we apply this kind of rule which was delivered to us in a similar way in other passages? Or as some wish, forsaking these things which such a great Apostle taught, should we turn again to "Jewish fables"? (Titus 1:14) It seems to me that if I differ from Paul in these matters I aid the enemies of Christ.

This is a telling description of the struggle in general—Are you for us or against us? Paul's way, in his spiritual interpretation of the Bible, is the path of truth, whereas the Jews err, according to Origen, in two directions: in their purely literal reading, as well as in their exegeses, which Paul had already called *Jewish fables* (or *myths* in the original Greek). In the middle of his sermon Origen says that between the Jewish fables and the simplistic readings is the path of truth; namely, the spiritual interpretation that brings together the Torah and the Gospel:[9] "See, therefore, to what extent the Gospel agrees with the Law... Cannot even the blind see clearly that one and the same Spirit wrote the Law and the Gospels?" Toward the end of the sermon Origen again tells his congregants that the Egyptians, masters of the world and spiritual evils, still invite the children of Israel to serve them, but those who have gone down to sea and cleansed themselves from sin will sing a new song.

So much for the external framework of the sermon, which allows us a glimpse into Origen's approach. Origen set himself two guidelines in his approach to Scripture. The first was that the meaning of the written text must be worthy of [*axion*] and appropriate to the God who gave it, as well as necessarily useful [*ophelein*] to the believer; while the second was that nothing in Scripture is meaningless, and the student benefits from every single detail.[10] Origen also spoke of three levels of exegesis. The first is "the literal level," the "historical" meaning, a basic layer that also entails some benefit. The second is the level intended to teach a moral lesson; whereas the final, highest level reveals mystical truths. Origen sees no drastic differences between the second and the last levels, nor does he attempt to exhaust all three levels in every individual comment.[11] Following is a discussion of the implementation of Origen's method in his fifth sermon on the book of Exodus.

Before commenting on the sojourn of the children of Israel in the desert, Origen explains to his audience the meaning of the *Hebrew* name of each place mentioned in the verse he is about to expound.[12] In his homily on the verses: "And the children of Israel journeyed from Rameses to Succoth"... "And they took their journey from Succoth and encamped in Etham (Exodus 12:37; 13:20), he states:[13]

> If there is anyone who is about to depart from Egypt, if there is anyone who desires to forsake the dark deeds of this world and the darkness of errors, he must first of all depart "from Ramesse." *Ramesse* means "the commotion of a moth." Depart from Ramesse, therefore, if you wish to come to this place that the Lord may be your leader, and precede you "in the column of the cloud" and "the rock" may follow you.... Nor should you store treasure "there where the moth destroys and thieves dig through and steal." (Matthew 6:20)

As for the content, this passage represents a typical move of Origen the homilist. Wishing to "uplift the souls"[14] of his listeners, he entreats them to forsake the accumulation of material goods, to leave behind the bustle of all that is transient. This is the first step in their own exodus from Egypt, a preparation for the spiritual life that, after going though the desert, will bring them to a new song.

As for the stylistic and literary dimensions of this sermon, they are no less important. The delicate transition from the Exodus in the distant past takes place right at the beginning, when Origen links the concept of the Exodus to another departure—"if there is anyone who desires to forsake the dark deeds of this world"—implying that the former exodus becomes a paradigm of the latter. Note that Origen then moves to the second person and turns to his audience directly. With great skill, he weaves in Paul's exegesis on the cloud and the rock, which he had developed in the preface to the sermon. He also resorts to an analogy to support his own interpretation—the Egyptian moth is the moth against which Jesus warns in Matthew. To conclude, he only needs a sentence to strengthen the tie linking Scripture and the Gospel:[15] "This is what the Lord says clearly in the Gospels: 'If you wish to be perfect, sell your possessions and give to the poor, and you will have treasure in heaven; and come, follow me.' (Matthew 19:21) This, therefore, is to depart 'from Ramesse' and to follow Christ. Let us see, however, what the campsites may be to which one goes 'from Ramesse.'" Anyone acquainted with rabbinic midrashim will probably see in these last two quotes, given their length as well as their level of literary development, a complete and appealing homily. The full surviving sermon, however, is almost ten times longer than these two passages together. Hence, it is not surprising that, on several occasions, Origen complains of restless audiences—"Some do not even patiently wait while the texts are being read in church. Others do not even know if they are read, but are occupied with mundane stories in the furthest corners of the Lord's house."[16]

Although he is sensitive to the attention of his audience, Origen is not deterred from tackling a completely new issue at the end of the sermon—an ancient tradition about the parting of the Red Sea. This legend, which is also found in rabbinic midrashim, tells us that the Holy One, blessed be He, "divided the Red Sea asunder" (Psalms 136:13) and set up a separate course for each tribe.[17] What is interesting are Origen's reasons for this addition:[18] "I thought that the careful student should not be silent about these things observed by the ancients in the divine Scriptures." The sermon on the Exodus from Egypt, about ten pages long, ends as follows:

> For he who does not do "the works of darkness" (Romans 13:12) destroys the Egyptian; he who lives not carnally but spiritually destroys the Egyptian; he who either casts out of his heart all sordid and impure thoughts or does not receive them at all destroys the Egyptian.... In this way, therefore, we can "see" even today, "the Egyptians dead and lying on the shore".... We can see Pharao himself drowned if we live by such faith that "God may quickly grind Satan under our feet" (cf. Rom. 16, 20) by Jesus Christ our Lord, "to whom belongs glory and sovereignty forever and ever. Amen."

The noticeable rhetorical effort in the last passage contrasts with the more scholarly or instructive tone we saw earlier. Origen scholars claim that he chose a relatively simple rhetorical style and, unlike some of his later followers, was not partial to the frills known to him from his classical studies.[19] At the end of the sermon Origen addresses an impassioned plea to the listener (or the reader!), mentioning the death of the Egyptians three times and including a prayer for the death of Satan, which adds a dramatic note to the concluding formula—the doxology.

As an interim summary, we must stress that Origen's sermon was cast in the form of an allegorical interpretation,[20] aiming to create a bridge between the textual source and the listener. Origen does not feel bound to expound the text sequentially, but dwells on the details of the story and on those exegeses required to give color and depth to the moral and spiritual points of his instruction. The whole sermon is imbued by a sense of movement and progress, inspired by the description of the biblical journey. Origen knows how to achieve this sense of progress and ascent, even when the topic at hand is not as well suited to his purpose.[21] On several occasions, Origen addresses his listeners (and readers) directly, with fervent requests to abide by the moral of the sermon in their behavior. The general public probably found this sermon too long and hard to follow, explaining why Origen laments that members of his congregation had tried to avoid these events. My feeling is that this is a genuine sermon, which was delivered in this form to an audience in Caesarea and transcribed on the spot by the stenographers placed at Origen's disposal for this purpose.[22] Origen may well have rewritten it or changed it but, in the main, this is a genuine sermon rather than a literary piece. When discussing rabbinic midrashim later, we will have to remember that the technique of stenography, which was relatively new, was unavailable to the rabbis even if only because they preached most of their sermons on days when writing was forbidden (such as sabbaths and holidays). We should also point out that in rabbinic midrashim, in contrast with Origen's preaching, the audience is almost never addressed directly.

Two other sermons, the sixth and seventh, deal with the song at the sea and the waters at Mara, and this will complete the

picture of the Exodus. The seventh sermon is the bluntest in its
open polemic with, and provocation of, the Jews. One of the
reasons for this is certainly the need to expound the central verse:
"there he made for them a statute and an ordinance" (Exodus
15:25). Already in the preface Origen wonders: "Was there not
another place more worthy, more fit, more fruitful, than that place
of bitterness" for God to give laws? He immediately answers—
indeed there was:[23] "I think that the Law, if it be undertaken
according to the letter, is sufficiently bitter and is itself Mara. For
what is so bitter as for a child to receive the wound of circumcision
on the eighth day and tender infancy suffer the hardness of the
iron?"

Origen then follows the text of the story and tells us that the
tree thrown into the water made the water sweet. For him, this tree
is none other than the "tree of life," the secret of the cross. Since the
Jews do not believe in this secret, they "are even now at Mara."[24]
The sermon then moves on to the story of the manna, and Origen
argues that the key to understanding this story is the fact that it
takes place on the "fifteenth day of the second month"—the
second Passover. As we know, the Bible (Numbers 9:9–11) sets a
second Passover for those who shall be "unclean by reason of a
dead body, or be on a journey afar off" and cannot celebrate the
Passover on its date. Origen stresses they are actually the ones who
benefited since, together with the feast of Passover, they were
blessed with manna. Who celebrates the second Passover if not the
Christians, who were unclean by reason of a dead body because
they were idolaters? Furthermore, the manna began to fall on
Sunday, the day of the Lord. Israel were told to gather the manna
during six days and then observe the sabbath! For Origen, this
clearly signaled that only Sundays are blessed, rather than the
sabbaths of the Jews.

It is hard to avoid the conclusion that Origen is waging a full-
scale war here against his Jewish rivals. The arguments do not
seem academic, and the zeal seems directed to crush the Jewish
adversary with uncontestable evidence.[25] As we mentioned in
Chapter 1, Origen wrote a whole treatise on the Passover sacrifice
based on the correct interpretation of the Hebrew word *Pesah*,
saying that Jews ridiculed Christians who had relied on a mistaken

understanding of the word in their disputes with them.[26] The feeling is that of a sharp, bitter polemic.

I have tried to illustrate how Origen opens up a new chapter in the rivalry between Christians and Jews; a Christian, combining exegetic discipline with passionate faith, expounds Scripture with a skill that must have impressed even his rivals. We will now turn to the exegetic skills of the Jews who opposed Origen.

The basic components of the homiletic endeavor—exegeses, word play, and contextual insight—are quite similar in both religious traditions. Thus, for instance, on the story of Mara, we find a commentary almost identical to that suggested by Origen in the *Mekhilta de-Rabbi Ishmael:*[27] "R. Simon B. Johai says: He showed him a teaching of the Torah. For it says: 'And the Lord taught him [*vayorehu*] a tree...' The *dorshe reshumot* say: He showed him words of the Torah which is likened to a tree, as it is said: 'She is a tree of life to them that lay hold upon her' (Proverbs 3:18)." Our concern is not with these basic constituent elements but with their general configuration and the way in which they constellate in the rabbinic approach. Let us first consider the differences between Origen's work and Jewish Midrash. First and foremost, a work that carries the personal imprint of an individual differs from an anthology. Origen also draws from other sources but, unlike a compilation of works by several authors and lacking a clear personal mark, he integrates them into his own teachings. Even if the compiler of an anthology selects only those homilies compatible with his own approach and stamps them with his own ideological bias, the work will still differ from that of an individual author. For instance, the most carefully edited of all rabbinic anthologies—*Leviticus Rabbah*—has none of the dramatic movement suffusing Origen's work. At least two of the stylistic elements used by Origen are absent: the direct address to the audience, and the connecting links between the various homilies. This is clearly not due to lack of skill; rather, it indicates that the literary aims of the Midrash differed from those of Origen. Due consideration should also be given to the fact that the midrashic anthology usually viewed as the homiletic midrash par excellence lacks a classic style of homiletic rhetoric.

What do we know about rhetoric in rabbinic times? Have any speeches or actual sermons been preserved that could serve as a basis of comparison with midrashic material? From the beginning of the *Wissenschaft des Judentums* in the nineteenth century, midrashic literature was conceptualized in Leopold Zunz's important work *Die gottesdienstlichen Vorträge der Juden historisch entwickelt*[28] within the framework of the public sermon and the religious oration. A century and a quarter later, J. Heinemann expanded this approach in his studies about the public sermon.[29] Recently, many scholars have shunned this approach and opted for that suggested by I. Heinemann in his classic work *Darkhei ha-Aggadah*. This scholarly tendency is reflected in two trends: one is the perception of Midrash as, first and foremost, the exegesis of Scripture,[30] and the other is the emphasis on the careful literary editing of some midrashic works.[31] Indeed, the comparison with Origen seems to support the view of later scholars, who minimized the importance of the live sermon. The question, however, remains: What do we know about sermons or rhetoric in rabbinic times?[32]

When discussing this topic, Lieberman relied on evidence from a homily in *Leviticus Rabbah*, of which he says: "The comments on the biblical verses, regarding both style and contents, varied according to the audience the preacher had before him.... The preacher's approach to his two audiences speaks for itself."[33]

In another article, with his inimitable insight, Lieberman was able to pinpoint the sabbath on which R. Meir delivered a sermon reported in PT Hagiga 2:1 (77b) and in parallel versions, on the basis of the verses expounded.[34] These two examples, however, are included in amoraic works and, furthermore, in no way are they rhetorically different from other homilies found in midrashic anthologies, either early or later ones.

It is thus apparently the case, that we have relatively few "live" sermons dating from the tannaitic period and included in a tannaitic anthology. Following is a rare example of such a "tannaitic" sermon, seemingly transcribing a live event, although it was preserved in only a relatively late midrash. The story is about R. Akiva's students, who gathered in Usha after Bar Kokhba's rebellion and delivered sermons in honor of their hosts at the end of their assembly. The following is the last of these sermons (*Song of Songs Rabbah* 2):[35]

R. Eliezer b. Jacob then came forward and expounded: "And Moses and the priests the Levites spoke unto all Israel, saying: Keep silence, and hear, O Israel; this day thou art become a people" (Deut. 27:9). Was it then on that day that they received the Torah? Had they not already received the Torah forty years before? How then can you say, "this day"? It teaches you, however, that since Moses had taught (repeated) to them the Torah and they had received it gladly, it was accounted to them as if they had received it that day from Mount Sinai. Therefore it is said, "This day thou art become a people to the Lord thy God." To you then, our brethren, children of Usha, who have received our teachers so gladly, how much more does this apply!

The finale distinguished this passage from the familiar structure of rabbinic sermons. In the middle we find familiar elements—questions, nuances on a verse, and a moral in the style of "it teaches you," all conventional features of Midrash. The true innovation is obviously the direct appeal to a specific audience "to you, then, our brethren, men of Usha." It seems self-evident that a preacher embarking on a fund-raising drive or attempting to console mourners would include in his sermon words of praise or comfort for the local people, as in the sermon to the people of Usha.

Another classic instance of rhetoric in a tannaitic anthology appears in the renowned, dreadful story about a murder in the Temple, although midrashic acuity is not the most prominent feature of this story. We read in the *Tosefta*, *Kippurim* 1:12:

There were two priests running up the ramp, and one shoved the other within four cubits; he took a knife and stabbed him in the heart. R. Zadok came and stood on the steps of the Rams (ms. variant-"hall") and said: "Hear me our brethren, the House of Israel. Scripture says, 'If in the land...any one is found slain...then your elders and your judges shall come forth and they shall measure the distance.' Come let us measure for whom we should sacrifice the calf, for the sanctuary or for the courts." And all wailed...

The direct appeal to the public—"Hear me our brethren, the House of Israel" brings the desirable emotional response at the end of the story. Note the recurring use of the expression "our brethren," a standard form of address in speeches (as found here and earlier) and in letters.[36] This formulation is conspicuously absent in rabbinic midrashim.

Many exegeses of biblical verses may have emerged in a homiletical-rhetorical context. However, because they reached their final form only in the midrashic medium, they were sapped of the vitality and intimacy of a direct appeal and fashioned in a uniform pattern, common to all midrashim. It is not my claim that the difference between Origen and the sages is the difference between Greek rhetoric and rabbinic midrash. Rather, it seems that the rabbis, just like Origen, resorted to one style when preaching in public and another when writing biblical commentaries. Their oral work, however, the live sermon, was not preserved in the Midrash, and only a midrashic-exegetic skeleton has survived. These remnants are deposited in midrashic anthologies, next to "proper" homilies and commentaries originating in the rabbinic academies where the sages interpreted Scripture to their students.

It is important and interesting to note that traces of live rhetoric, or imitations of it, are actually more prevalent in halakhic literature. *Midreshei halakha*, for instance, precede alternative interpretations with such formulations as "you say so," or "rather, it is," or "you are making an a fortiori judgment," which gave a live and dialogical rhythm to the midrash.[37] In this context, note the frank and intense exchange between R. Eliezer, R. Joshuah, and R. Akiva in M. Pesahim 6:2, including R. Eliezer's amazement at his friend R. Joshua—"What is this, Joshua! How can a voluntary act be any proof concerning an obligatory act!"—and at his disciple R. Akiva—"Akiva, wouldest thou uproot what is written in the Torah!" Actually the halakhic realm, then, contains more traces of live oral creativity than the midrashic literature devoted to Aggada.[38]

Evidence of public sermons, or rather stories about them, in which the hero of the story is sometimes a *tanna*, appear in amoraic literature. Besides the story in the Palestinian Talmud about R. Meir's sermon in the Tiberias study house on the sabbath, mentioned previously, we have another story about him in PT Sotah, reporting that R. Meir used to preach in Hamat, near Tiberias, on Friday evening. Once, although his sermon lasted much longer, a woman who was "used to hearing his voice" remained and returned home after the candle had gone out, to an exasperated husband who had waited up for her.[39] In *Genesis Rabbah*, and in the parallel version in *Pesikta de-Rav Kahana*,[40] we are told that R. Simeon b. Yohai's three students "asked permission" to depart by expounding verses before him (as was the custom on such occasions). There is also a charming story from the first generation of amoraim about people rushing to hear a sermon by R. Yohanan, and the elderly R. Hanina's pride in having taught R. Yohanan this skill:[41] "R. Hanina was supporting himself on R. Hiyya bar Aba in Sepphoris, and saw all the people running. He said to him: 'Why are they running?' Said he: 'R. Yohanan is teaching at the study house of R. Benaiah, and all the people are running to hear him.' Said he: 'Blessed be the Merciful One who shows me my fruits while I am yet alive. I have taught him all the Aggada, except for Proverbs and Ecclesiastes.'" A similar description of Jews crowding to hear a sermon and their enthusiasm, exaggerated in his eyes, appears in the writings of Jerome, a fourth-century Church Father.[42] Indirectly, the story in the Palestinian Talmud suggests that there were two levels in the exegesis of Scripture—the "private" lessons that R. Hanina gave his disciple R. Yohanan, and the public sermon, which appears to be a more popular form.

These few places notwithstanding, tannaitic literature contains almost no evidence of a contemporary live sermon. Perhaps the most poignant example is in Tosefta Sotah 7:9 and deserves special attention:[43]

> R. Yohanan b. Berokah and R. Eliezer Hisma came from Yavne to Lod and greeted R. Joshua in Peki 'in. Said R. Joshua to them: "What was new in the study house today?" Said they: "We are your disciples and drink of your waters." Said he: "It is impossible that nothing new was said in the house of study. Whose Sabbath was it?" Said they: "It was the Sabbath of R. Elazar b. Azariah." Said he: "And what was the *haggadah*?" Said they: "'Assemble the people, men, women and children'." (Deuteronomy 31:12) Said he: "And how did he expound it?" Said they: "Rabbi, this is how he expounded: 'The men came to study and the women came to listen, why

did the children come? To ensure a reward to those who brought them'. And he also expounded: 'You have declared this day concerning the Lord' (Deut. 26:17–18) and he also expounded: 'The sayings of the wise are like goads.' (Eccl. 12:11) Should someone say in his thoughts, since the House of Shammai declare unclean and the House of Hillel clean, so-and-so prohibits and so-and-so permits, why should I learn Torah any longer? Scripture says, 'words', 'the words', 'these are the words' (Deuteronomy 1:1): all these words have been given by one Shepherd, one God created them, one Provider gave them, the Lord of all deeds, blessed be He, has spoken them. So you too, make many chambers in your heart and place in them the words of the House of Hillel and the words of the House of Shammai, the words of those who declare unclean and the words of those who declare clean'." He said to them: "A generation is not orphaned when R. Eleazar dwells among them."

After the opening civilities, where students declare loyalty to R. Joshua, their rabbi, and his teachings, they are asked three questions concerning the study in Yavneh: (1) "Whose Sabbath was it?"; (2) "What was the Haggada?"; namely, what verses were expounded. (3) "And how did he expound it?"; what were the contents of the teaching?

I will not enter into a comprehensive literary analysis of this source and will only point out the considerable tension between the teaching in Yavneh and R. Joshua's absence from there. Although the first homily stresses that the whole people—men, women, and children—should come together at the gathering, the last one indicates that we must become adept in all methods, as all "were given by one Shepherd." This is possible only when all are brought together. R. Joshua's answer, too—"a generation is not orphaned"—appears to be ironic, as if he were saying that it is good for this generation to have a leader who brings together men, women, and children. Although R. Joshua's words could also be viewed as praise, I find this interpretation less appealing. To return to our main concern, narrative evidence of sermons preached at a gathering of sages in Yavneh, perhaps even on the sabbath, is now

available. This homily ends with a direct appeal to the listener—
"you too, make many chambers in your heart...," which, as we
saw, is quite exceptional.

This tannaitic tradition, and others resembling it, deserves
further research. Through the comparison with Origen we have
tried to look at midrashic anthologies in a new light and concluded
that, in their present shape, they are the product of an editing
process intended to preserve commentaries and exegeses on
Scripture. It is not thereby implied, however, that biblical exegesis
originates and grows solely through this process or only within
this social context. At least some of the homilies included in these
midrashic anthologies were, indeed, public sermons, of their times
and for their times, whereas only the hard core of the homily—the
exegesis of the verse—has been preserved for posterity. We need to
develop criteria for evaluating how these various units came into
being—whether as a scholarly commentary on a verse or as a
public sermon. In Chapter 9 we deal with Jerome's commentary on
Ecclesiastes, which will shed further light on the development and
influence of a work wholly devoted to biblical exegesis.

8

Love and Holiness: The Midrash on Song of Songs and Origen's Homilies

The Song of Songs enjoyed singularly good fortune. Not only was this unique book included in the biblical canon, but it was also deemed to have an added measure of holiness that set it apart from and above the rest of Scripture. It was R. Akiva who championed the uniqueness of the Song, in the context of a discussion about its canonical status. Some tannaim among R. Akiva's disciples (R. Yose) and friends (Simeon b. Uzzai) suggested that the question of whether the Song of Songs does "render the hands unclean," a feature characterizing the rest of Scripture,[1] had been a point of contention. R. Akiva vehemently protests against the very possibility of any such dispute ever having arisen (M. Yadaim 3:5):[2] "God forbid!—no man in Israel ever disputed about the Song of Songs [that he should say] that it does not render the hands unclean, for the entire world is not worth the day on which the Song of Songs was given to Israel; for all the Writings [Ketubim] are holy, but the Song of Songs is the Holy of Holies."

This chain of arguments requires an explanation. The last argument is R. Akiva's statement that the Song of Songs surpasses all other "Writings." It seems plausible that *Writings* should be seen here in its broad meaning—Scripture or biblical verses—rather than in the narrow connotation of Hagiographa (as opposed to the Torah and the Prophets).[3] Even if we take the narrow view of the term *writings*, which I do not accept, R. Akiva's first argument suffices to confer special status on the Song of Songs. After all, R. Akiva speaks of the day when the Song of Songs was "given" to Israel—literally, in the same phrase used for the "giving" of the Torah itself. The day when the Song of Songs was given was a day of revelation, "worthier" than the entire world; it is a day of entry into the most inner sanctum—the Holy of Holies.[4]

Why did R. Akiva praise the Song of Songs so highly? The conventional view is aptly formulated by Urbach: "It seems that this declaration [that the Song of Songs is the Holy of Holies] is linked to the mystical interpretation of the Song of Songs, which perceived this text as a description of the human soul's intense love and longing for God's presence, yearning to penetrate the mystical secrets and attain knowledge of the *Merkabah*."[5] This point seems to require further clarification. Two issues are combined in Urbach's view, though they need not be tied together. The first is the loving yearning of the believer to be close to God or, in the Psalmist's words, "As for me, nearness to God is good; I have made the Lord God my refuge." During the time of the Temple this longing was expressed in the hope to be sheltered in God's house: "One thing have I desired of the Lord, that will I seek after; that I may dwell in the house of the Lord all the days of my life..." (Psalms 27:4). After the destruction of the Temple, and possibly even earlier, while the Temple was still standing, God's presence was marked by a concern with His writings, and in the language of the Mishnah in Avot: "If ten men sit together and occupy themselves in the law, the *Shekinah* rests between them.... And whence even of one? Because it is written, 'In every place where I record my name I will come unto thee and I will bless thee' (3:6)."[6] These religious feelings are not necessarily "mystical." A mystical approach may come to the fore in a particular form of study, or through other devices meant to bring the believer "closer" to God, and according to other methods, even "unite" that believer with God.[7]

This distinction between love of God as a normative religious value as opposed to a mystical experience is very important when coming to evaluate R. Akiva's words. It could be claimed that R. Akiva is attempting to exalt the element of love in religion, which finds its most sublime expression in this book. The same R. Akiva for whom "you shalt love thy neighbor as thyself" is a "a great commandment of the Torah" is the R. Akiva who rejoiced at the chance to abide by "thou shalt live they God with all thy heart, and with all thy soul, and with all thy might," when he died as a martyr. It is thus possible that R. Akiva's praise for the Song of Songs is meant to stress the importance of love in his philosophy of religion. I show later that the concept of love was paramount in

Christianity from its inception. For now, suffice it to say that special status could definitely be conferred on the Song of Songs without resorting to mystical interpretations.[8]

Many scholars,[9] however, believe that the background of R. Akiva's statement is mystical contemplation or the mystical interpretations that accompanied the Song of Songs. Although Urbach tried to cull remnants of exegeses on the Song of Songs that are either mystical in character or concerned with mystical topics,[10] the truth is that the evidence for this relies on a few, isolated examples. The prevalent line in tannaitic literature is to expound the Song of Songs as concerned with the Exodus, as does the *Mekhilta*, or with the revelation at Sinai, or with future redemption, as does the *Sifre*.[11] *Song of Songs Rabbah* is similarly inclined and tends to understand the Song of Songs as a description of the giving of the Torah.[12] Another midrashic work on Song of Songs is *Song of Songs Zuta* ("Minor" Songs of Songs) or *Aggadat Shir Ha-Shirim*, which some scholars tend to see as an ancient text, dating back possibly to the end of the tannaitic period.[13] This work includes several clear references to subjects close to the mystical literature of the *Merkabah* circle. These references include the following texts in *Song of Songs Zuta*: "the lion and the bull in the *merkabah*, and peace is between them, in mutual love" (Schechter edn., line 145); "'the king has brought me into his chambers'—it teaches us that the Holy One, blessed be He, will show Israel the celestial secrets hidden in the chambers of heaven" (298–311); "And God tears the heavens and shows Israel the heavenly throne" (1134); "And the glory of Israel will break like fire from under the heavenly throne" (1334).[14]

Lieberman goes even further and concludes:

And we have already shown above that the basic revelation of God in His image in His *Merkabah*, on the sea, and at Mount Sinai is a *tannaitic* tradition, and these are *mishnahs*. The Song of Songs praises and exalts the Holy One, blessed be He, and His image, as it were, and also comments on the *Merkabah*... I now accept Scholem's assumption that the *mishnah*...of *Shi 'ur Komah* is an ancient homily on Song of Songs 5:10–19, included in an early *midrash* on the Song of

Songs.... In sum, besides the literal interpretation of Song of Songs there was in Israel an interpretation of this book, "which is inscribed in the true record".... Thus the midrash on the Song of Songs, and the *ma 'aseh Merkabah* and the *Shi'ur Komah* are one and the same.[15]

The special holiness of the Song of Songs, then, is not only linked to an allegorical understanding, which views it as a song of love between Israel and God,[16] but also as containing God's most arcane secrets; namely, His *Shi'ur Koma*. We will now consider Origen's approach to the Song of Songs and will then compare some of his homilies to the Midrash. This comparison follows a series of studies on this subject conducted by various scholars[17] and will enable us to review the course of comparative research and its development.

Origen's prolific opus includes a ten-volume commentary on the Song of Songs, written in the years 245–247 in Athens and Caesarea, and sermons on this book, which Origen scholars claim were preached in Caesarea between 239–242.[18] Less than half of his exegetical work on Song of Songs has survived, and both works—the exegesis and the sermons—cover almost up to the end of Chapter Two of the Song. Furthermore, only the Latin translation of these works has survived. Jerome translated the sermons in 383 C.E.; Rufinus, his rival, did the commentary in Jerusalem at the beginning of the fifth century.

In a seminal article, Elizabeth Clark pointed out Origen's purpose in his works on the Song of Songs, claiming that his main concern was the attitude of Christianity to Judaism.[19] Often, Origen refers to the Law that was given as a present to the bride, Israel, as a forerunner of the direct gift it received from Jesus. Clark argues that Origen struggles, on the one hand, against the gnostic threat that denies the Torah altogether and, on the other hand, against the Jewish repudiation of the messianic Gospel.[20] Yet, as Clark herself admits,[21] the topic that captivated readers and scholars in Origen's exegesis was his reading of the Song as describing the soul's relationship to Jesus and its mystical ascent.

In the first pages of his introduction Origen warns his readers not to climb to the lofty heights of the Song unless they have thoroughly prepared themselves. For those who live "only after the flesh," reading the Song may be dangerous.[22] Their carnal passions may be aroused, and they may come to believe that their reading of the Bible has encouraged this. Interestingly, Origen relies on Jewish custom for his warning regarding the study of the Song, claiming "we have received from them":[23]

> For they say that with the Hebrews also care is taken to allow no one even to hold this book in his hands, who has not reached a full and ripe age. And there is another practice too that we have received from them—namely, that all the Scriptures should be delivered to boys by teachers and wise men, while at the same time the four that they call *deuteroseis*—that is to say, the beginning of Genesis, in which the creation of the world is described; the first chapters of Ezekiel, which tell about the cherubim; the end of that same, which contains the building of the Temple; and this book of the Song of Songs—should be reserved for study till the last.

Should the Jewish ban, if Origen's information is indeed accurate and reliable, be ascribed to the mystical status of the book, as is true for the stories of the Creation and the *Merkabah*? Or should we transpose Origen's apprehensions as quoted previously and argue that Jews too were actually afraid of the sexual connotations of this text![24] In the rest of the introduction Origen considers the mystical features of the book, and his approach deserves our attention.

Origen's introduction includes five sections. In the first he warns the readers, as just mentioned. In the second he demonstrates, relying on Paul, that the two creation stories in Genesis symbolize the outer and inner man, and the Bible uses the language of bodily members to describe both. In this fashion, Origen sets the ground for explaining the carnal expressions in the Song of Songs as alluding to the inner, spiritual man rather than to the carnal love of the outer one.[25] The third part of the introduction is an important, lengthy essay on the place of love in Scripture. Origen proves that the Bible generally refrains from using the word *Eros*, that is, sexual passion, even when the context demands it (as in the story of Amnon and Tamar), and prefers the softer term

Agape. One exception is Proverbs 4:6–8, where we are told about wisdom—(in the Septuagint translation): "Desire her greatly, and she shall preserve thee; encompass her, and she shalt exalt thee; honor her, that she may embrace thee." The Septuagint does not recoil from the use of the *erastes*, because the aim of this all-consuming passion is totally clear.[26] Origen's approach is quite unique even within the Church, which so emphasized the value of love in religion.[27] He believed "it is impossible for human nature not to be always feeling the passion of love for something,"[28] and aimed to direct the fire of love to its most sublime and appropriate object, love for God. It is almost obvious that Origen's first quotation after this statement should be Matthew 22:34–40, where Jesus answers that the first great commandment is "You shall love the Lord thy God" and the second is "You shall love thy neighbor as thyself."[29] We could attempt here to distinguish between love for God, which Origen preaches, and mysticism, except that Origen himself speaks here of mystical contemplation, as we learn from the next section in the introduction.

In the fourth part of the introduction, Origen discusses the place of the Song of Songs against the backdrop of two other books by Solomon included in the biblical canon, Proverbs and Ecclesiastes.[30] He compares the latter two to the study of ethics and nature, which he views as a necessary stage that must precede the contemplation of the invisible and stresses that the Greeks had borrowed a similar, tripartite division from Solomon.[31] At that point, whoever has prepared himself and cleansed his soul in all its actions and habits "is competent to proceed on dogmatic and mystical matters, and in this way advances to the contemplation of the Godhead with pure and spiritual love."[32] Origen's language at the end of the previous section of the introduction, dealing with love, also points, even if not explicitly, in a mystical direction: "The Scripture before us... sings by the Spirit the song of the marriage whereby the Church is joined and allied to Christ the heavenly Bridegroom, desiring to be united to Him through the Word."[33] Scholars also concur in noting that, as we proceed, the mystical overtones in Origen's exegesis of the Song of Songs become more and more pronounced.[34] In other words, Origen's perception of this book as a mystical voyage, and his explicit mention of the book's special place in the Jewish curriculum, encourages us to support Scholem's and Lieberman's view that mystical perception of the Song of Songs was prevalent.

The links between Origen's view and the rabbinic interpretation become even more obvious in the fifth and last part of the introduction and in Origen's commentaries preserved in both his works—the exegesis and the homilies on the Song of Songs. The last part of the introduction deals with the first verse of the Song of Songs and dwells on the words, while comparing it to Solomon's two other books. Origen raises the following points:

1. The Song of Songs is the finest of poems, preferable to all the biblical songs that preceded it (of which he enumerates six, beginning with the song at the sea, while the Song of Songs is the seventh) and even to those that followed it (such as the song of Isaiah).[35]
2. The Song of Songs is the only one of Solomon's three books, all of which "served the will of the Holy Spirit" (p. 51), where neither the place where he reigns nor his ancestry is mentioned at all (pp. 53–54). The reason for this is that this Song describes the union with the perfection of all things, which takes place after everything becomes subject to God, whose name then becomes Solomon [*Shelomo*], to whom peace [*shalom*] is given. In Origen's method, Solomon is obviously a type, a symbol of Jesus.
3. Some scholars, who have suggested that the Song of Songs is the most special of *Solomon's* songs, rely on evidence from I Kings 5:12—"and his poems were a thousand and five." Origen dismisses this possibility saying that neither the Church nor the Hebrews, "by whom God's utterances were transmitted to us," (p. 55) have preserved Solomon's other songs or included them in the Bible.

In *Song of Songs Zuta* we find the following points in the discussion of the book's first verse:

1. There are ten songs, the song of Adam, the song of Abraham, the song of the sea...and the song of the world to come, "sing to the Lord a new song," and the Song of Songs is the choicest of all. (Schechter edn., lines 195–196)[36]

2. R. Gamaliel says, the Holy God, blessed be He, said it, as we are told—the choicest of all songs... Who said it? He whose is peace, and conducts peace on His creatures. (lines 3–5)[37]

3. To tell you how great are Solomon's gifts. It is said of Solomon "And he spoke three thousand proverbs: and his poems were a thousand and five" and the Song of Songs is the finest.

Origen's knowledge of Jewish tradition concerning the book's holiness may lend credence to the possibility that, in his introduction, Origen relied on the Jewish sources he quoted from *Song of Songs Zuta* and on others,[38] adapting them to his purpose.

Scholars have labored much to show the mutual influences between Origen and the rabbis concerning the exegesis of the second verse—"Let him kiss me with the kisses of his mouth"—to which we turn now. The first task is to examine the interpretation of *Song of Songs Rabbah*, and seek its sources and parallels within rabbinic literature. This is a vital step before turning to comparisons with outside sources, to preclude hasty hypotheses about possible influences between the two religions. *Song of Songs Rabbah* views the first verse as relating to the revelation at Sinai[39] and brings a dispute between R. Yohanan and the rabbis. We juxtapose these two approaches:

> "Another explanation: Let him kiss
> me with the kisses of his mouth":

R. Yohanan said: An angel carried the dibber [or utterance at Mount Sinai] from before the Holy One, in turn, and brought it to each of the Israelites and said to him, "Do you take upon yourself this commandment? So-and-so many rules are attached	The rabbis, however, say: "The dibber [utterance] itself went in turn to each one of the Israelites and said...

to it, so-and-so many penalties
are attached to it, so many enacted
prohibitions and so many precepts,
inferences from minor to major are
attached to it; such-and-such
a reward is attached to it."
The Israelite would answer him,
"Yes." He then said, "Do you
accept the divinity of the Holy
One, blessed be he?" and he
answered, "Yes, yes." Thereupon   ...and straightaway the
he kissed him on the mouth;   commandment kissed him on
hence it says, "To thee it was   the mouth...."[40] Hence it
shown that thou mightest know   is written "Lest thou forget
that the Lord is God," namely,   the things which thine eyes
by an [angelic] messenger.   saw."

Both approaches stress that the revelation at Sinai was a process of conscious acceptance by "each one of the Israelites" but differ on the measure of hypostasis, or substance, ascribed to "the utterance." The rabbis believed that the utterance could reveal itself to the people of Israel, while R. Yohanan believed that an angel brought the word of God to the people and explained it. This is an interesting dispute, and the link between the rabbis' perception of the utterance and that of the *logos* in nonrabbinic systems has already been discussed.[41] The thrust of both approaches, however, that of R. Yohanan and that of the rabbis, is to turn the revelation at Sinai into an official ceremony of acceptance, as is conveyed by the tannaitic source on which both these homilies rely.

The verse in Deuteronomy 32:10 (the song of Moses)—"He compassed him about, he cared for him, he kept him as the apple of his eye"—is expounded as follows:[42]

"He compassed him about"—before Mount Sinai, as it is said, "And thou shalt set bounds unto the people round about." "He cared for him"—through the Ten Commandments. This teaches that when the utterance [*dibber*] came forth from the mouth of the Holy One, blessed be He, Israel saw it, per-

ceived it, and knew how many interpretations were contained in it, how many laws were contained in it, how many
inferences from the minor to the major were contained in it,
how many analogies were in it.

This beautiful tannaitic homily may be seen as the raw material
used in the creation of both the later homilies—that of R. Yohanan
and that of the rabbis. This is a short and elegant explanation of
"he cared for him," describing the measure of knowledge attained
by Israel at the Sinai revelation. They understood the complete
utterance, in all its implications. This source is very hard to date,
and it could well have been written at the end of the tannaitic
period, close to Origen's times. We can assume, however, that it
preceded the homily of R. Yohanan, who then went on to develop
it. When we return to *Song of Songs Rabbah*, we will see that both
homilies attempt to stress the full and willing participation of the
people of Israel in accepting the Torah. The description is that of a
formal legal procedure, where the people of Israel actually sign
that they consent to the Torah and accept the Holy One, blessed be
He, as their God. Is this a reflection of a ritual of consent during the
amoraic period, perhaps even of a conversion practice common in
Palestine, which the homilist "projected" backward to describe the
acceptance of the Torah by the people of Israel? This is merely a
conjecture, but a similar homily in *Leviticus Rabbah*, also quoted in
R. Yohanan's name, describes the Sinai revelation as a formal legal
process: "R. Yohanan said: They [i.e., God and Israel] gave recip-
rocal promises: He—that He would not deny them, they—that
they would not deny Him. R. Isaac said: When one administers an
oath to his legions, he does so with a sword, the implication being:
Whoever transgresses these conditions, let the sword pass over his
neck."[43] Lieberman preferred the *Leviticus Rabbah* version, which
reads *orkomosia* rather than *compromissum*, and argued that this
passage is intended to mean "swearing to a treaty."[44] R. Yohanan,
then, tends to describe the Sinai revelation as a mutually binding
legal procedure, as we saw in *Leviticus Rabbah* and in *Song of Songs
Rabbah*. We can now consider Origen's view of Song of Songs and
the scholarly views of its links to Midrash mentioned earlier:

So it must be the Church as a corporate personality who speaks and says: "I am sated with the gifts which I received as bethrotal presents or as dowry before my marriage. For of old, while I was being prepared for my wedding with the King's Son and the Firstborn of all creation, His holy angels put themselves at my service and ministered to me, bringing the Law as a bethrotal gift; for "the Law," it is said, "was ordained by angels in the hand of a mediator" (Galatians 3:19).... But, since the age is almost ended and His own presence is not granted me, and I see only His ministers ascending and descending upon me, because of this I pour out my petition to Thee, the Father of my Spouse, beseeching Thee to have compassion at last upon my love, and to send Him, that He may now no longer speak to me only by His servants the angels and the prophets, but may come Himself, directly, and kiss me with the kisses of His mouth—that is to say, may pour the words of His mouth into mine.[45]

Urbach draws the following conclusion from this passage: "Origen seems to have copied here R. Yohanan's first claim,[46] but also the second homily of the Jewish sage.[47] R. Yohanan is attempting to dismiss the anthropomorphic interpretation of the verse, by introducing an angel who kisses on the mouth every one in Israel who accepts the utterance. The Church Father expounds the mediation of the angels in derogatory terms and underscores the supremacy of the Church, which was kissed by the Christ."[48] In light of the development of the homily, it would appear that R. Yohanan is not concerned with the issue of mediation but with the formal agreement between Israel and God, resting on Israel's deep understanding of the Torah. If there is any polemic at all here, it hinges on the attempt to show that Israel has the deepest and most precise understanding of the Torah, including all its interpretations. Israel have signed an agreement attesting to their understanding and their faith, which are the best possible.

I have tried to show in this chapter that comparisons between the homiletic traditions of the two religions can be attempted only after charting the development of a particular homily in each religion separately. Only then can we estimate to what extent the homily is polemical. Abiding by this methodological stricture in a comparative work is trying. But if we trace the internal development of each homily within its own tradition, we will be rewarded when attempting to gauge its polemical potential.[49]

9

The Midrash on Ecclesiastes and Jerome's Commentary

As is well known, the brief reign of the Emperor Julian, "the Apostate"[1] is one of the last historical events mentioned in the Palestinian Talmud. Julian, who was raised as a Christian, tried to restore traditional Roman religion to the empire while eradicating the bane of Christianity, which had been a dominant force in the empire for close to forty years, since the days of Constantine and his son. Julian's hatred for Christianity led him to support Judaism and encourage the Jews to rebuild their temple in Jerusalem.[2] In his attempt to undermine the status of Christians in the empire, Julian wrote a full treatise devoted to this subject entitled *Against the Galileans*. Julian's efforts were foiled by his death in battle, in 363 C.E., only three years after he had ascended to the throne. The three years of his reign shook the Church and affected it far beyond the temporary hiatus in the process of Christianity's stride toward dominance under the aegis of the preceding emperors. The awareness that the tide could be turned proved to the church that the ancient roots of paganism still ran deep in the Roman empire. Furthermore, Julian's patronage of the Jews reawoke the potential threat that Judaism posed to Christian believers and spurred the Church to continue its campaign against Judaism, as well as against judaizers within the Church.

Jerome, the foremost biblical scholar of the Church in antiquity,[3] was still a schoolboy (as he himself noted in his commentary on Habakkuk) when news arrived of Julian's death. Jerome tells us that, on hearing of it, a pagan said it proved that the God of the Christians, rather than "long suffering" is a "swift avenger."[4] Jerome's grammar school was one of the most, if not *the* most, prestigious one in Rome.[5] Donatus, his famous teacher, instilled in his talented student a love for and an understanding of classical literature that Jerome sustained throughout his life, although he did recoil from it at a later stage and attempted to abandon it altogether. In his commentary on Ecclesiastes, written in Bethlehem twenty-five years later Jerome mentions his instructor in the classics when commenting on the verse "and there is nothing new under the sun" (1:9): "A similar idea was suggested by the comic poet: 'There's naught been said that's not been said before' [Terence, the prologue by Eunuchus]. Donatus, my instructor, when expounding this dictum, said: 'So the hell with those who've said it before me.'"[6] Jerome himself was criticized for abiding by this principle in his own exegeses and sermons. To say he was not always careful to credit the sources he used in his commentaries, or even to mention that he had used such sources, would be an understatement. Some of his own students, as well as some modern scholars, view him mainly as a collector and compiler[7] and consider his personal achievement negligible. Later scholars have tried to balance this perception, in my view correctly, and have stressed his unique contribution regarding both the scope of his sources and the unique talents he brought to the study of Scripture. Our study of Jerome's exegeses will allow us access to the main exegetical schools active in the church at the time. I will first consider Jerome's influence as an exegete and then discuss possible inferences that might be drawn from his work regarding rabbinic Midrash.

Jerome was born to a Christian family in Stridon, a northwestern region of what was then Italy and later northwestern Yugoslavia. His full name, Hieronymus Eusebius, attests to his Christian origins and means, in Greek, "of sacred name, devout."[8] We have already noted that he received an impeccable classical education. Christian families had entrusted imperial schools with providing their children with the background necessary for their religious instruction. Julian's ruling, therefore, forbidding Christians to study the classics, dealt a heavy blow to the Christian system of education.[9] Nevertheless, Jerome's studies did prepare him for desirable public posts in the empire. After graduating from Donatus' grammar school, apparently at the usual age of sixteen, and following his studies at the school of rhetoric, also in Rome, many doors could have opened up for him. As the Aramaic rabbinic saying tells us, however, a man's legs lead him to where he is needed. Jerome first devoted his Sundays to walk in the Roman catacombs, which were considered the burial places of martyrs. Before leaving Rome he was baptized,[10] and shortly after we find him secluded with monks in the Syrian desert. Jerome played an important role in the history of Christian monasticism. Indeed, the last thirty-five years of his life, as well as his productive years as a commentator and translator of Scripture, were spent in a monastery he founded in Bethlehem.

In addition to his ascetic experiences in the company of the monks in Syria, Jerome attests to have sought other ways of repressing his passions. He found these in the desert, where he devoted himself to the study of Hebrew with a Jewish convert to Christianity. Whatever the authenticity of this report, Jerome left the desert after three years of studying Hebrew, becoming acquainted with Syriac, and improving his Greek.[11] This brief biographical outline takes us to that chapter in Jerome's life where he meets the first of his teachers specializing in biblical exegesis. This teacher, together with others, is described by Jerome in a letter often quoted by scholars. The letter (84) was written c. 400 C.E.:[12]

> At Antioch I frequented the lectures of Apollinaris of Laodicea and I was much devoted to him. But even though he instructed me in the Holy Scriptures, I never accepted his disputable dogma on Christ's human mind. Later on, though my hair was already becoming gray, which is more becoming in a professor than in a pupil, I nevertheless journeyed to Alexandria and attended the lectures of Didymus. In many respects I gratefully acknowledge my debt to him. What I did not know I learnt; what I already knew I did not lose under his instruction. Then, when people thought I would finally call a halt to my schooling, I came back again to Jerusalem and Bethlehem, and there had Bar-anina teach me at night. With what trouble, too, and at what a cost! Far he was afraid of the Jews and used to come to me like another Nicodemus.

The rest of the letter is no less interesting than this passage, but I stop here to highlight the contribution of these three teachers.

The two teachers Apollinaris and Didymus are prominent representatives of two separate and even opposing schools of biblical exegesis in the ancient Church. Didymus the Blind of Alexandria wrote many commentaries using Origen's method. His endeavor was to grasp the spiritual-mystical meaning of Scripture (anagoge), and he often resorted to allegorical interpretations.[13] We will quote an example of his exegesis on Ecclesiastes and compare it with the approach of his rival Apollinaris.

The research into Didymus' writings acquired new impetus when a treasure trove of his writings was discovered at Tura, near Cairo, in 1941. The publication of his commentaries on Zechariah, Ecclesiastes, Job, and Psalms, based on these ancient papyri, began about twenty years later. His commentary on Ecclesiastes is supposed to have been written between 377 and 381, a few years before the publication of Jerome's commentary on the book (c. 389).[14] A very interesting point concerns the scholarly view of Didymus' commentary on Ecclesiastes. The prevalent perception is that this book is, in fact, a stenographic transcription of Didymus' lessons at his academy![15] In other words, this commentary faithfully captures Didymus' activity as a teacher. The possibility that we are actually reading the lectures Jerome attended during the time he spent studying with Didymus[16] is indeed fascinating. Let us take, for instance, Didymus' exegesis on Ecclesiastes 7:2: "It is better to go to the house of mourning, than to go to the house of feasting: for that is the end of all men; and the living will lay it to his heart." Following is Didymus' exegesis:[17]

> "It is better to go to the house of mourning, than to go to the house of feasting."

> Moral laxity is not found where there is mourning. There, mirth and laughter are shunned. The event itself precludes this... It is better, then, for the wise to go to the house of mourning than to go to the house of feasting. Drinking together, although not leading to evil, does not lead to good either.

> Question: Should we not see "mourning" as negative?

[Answer]: [What is meant here is] that [mourning] which is praised by the Savior. According to the literal level (*reton*) we say that…the house of mourning indicates that we are neither the first nor the only ones afflicted by this mourning—rather, mourning is shared by all.

Question: [And] the spiritual interpretation [anagoge]

[Answer]: A house is mourning where the moral beliefs of sinners have their punishment. On hearing of them, people…mourn and lament for themselves. This mourning, then, is good, as it brings praise. "Blessed are those who mourn, for they shall be comforted" (Matthew 5:4). The preamble and the beginning of comfort is mourning.

The "house" signifies [semenai] a situation or a behavior, not a place. For he knows "that is the end of all men; and the living will lay it to his heart." He who goes to the house of mourning knows that the end of every man is to die. And if he knows he will die, he will not appreciate or value greatly the acquisition of possessions, as the things he holds will be lost in his death—wealth, honor and fame—according to the verse "Be not thou afraid when one is made rich, when the glory of his house is increased; for when he dies he shall carry nothing away."[18]

This passage handsomely integrates a literal exegesis and a symbolic-allegorical one, when the latter follows naturally and pleasantly from the former. In the allegorical exegesis, the house of mourning comes to symbolize man lamenting his sins. In the end, however, Didymus returns to the literal level, stressing the moral implied in the finale of the Ecclesiastes verse and marshalling support from a verse in Psalms, as he had cited the New Testament to sustain his allegorical interpretation. His main message is that genuine mourning is for those who leave God, not for those who die and abandon this world.[19]

This is a typical, evocative example of the two levels of exegesis in Didymus, integrating the literal level and the anagoge, the allegory. Jerome later criticized Didymus for not being sufficiently meticulous in his literal interpretation and for being far too attracted

to symbolic exegesis.[20] Jerome doubtlessly agreed with Didymus'
reading of Ecclesiastes; after all, he himself had suggested to a
young virgin that she read Ecclesiastes so that she may "become
accustomed to tread underfoot the things of the world.[21] Indeed,
when writing his own commentary on Ecclesiastes, Jerome concludes his exegesis of the first verse by persistently denying that
Ecclesiastes carries a hedonistic message:[22] "Badly, then, do certain
people conjecture that we are stirred to pleasure and luxury by this
book because, on the contrary, everything which we perceive in
this world is shown to be vanities; nor ought we vigorously desire
these things which perish as soon as they are attained." But although he agrees with Didymus concerning the general message,
Jerome adheres to the method of Didymus' rival Apollinaris, by
carefully dwelling on the literal level before proceeding to consider
meaning. Furthermore, the commitment of the Antiochene school
to the literal interpretation of Scripture may well have been the
dominant factor in Jerome's later interest in Hebrew exegesis,
which culminated in his conviction that the Hebrew text was the
true version of Scripture and preferable to the Septuagint. We will
show something of the Antiochene method as it comes to the fore
in the work of Apollinaris, which is preserved only in the later
catena.[23]

Jerome mentions his teacher Apollinaris about forty times.[24]
One of these references, a relatively long one, appears in Jerome's
exegesis on Ecclesiastes 4:13–16: "Better is a poor and wise child
than an old and foolish king.... I saw all the living.... There is no
end of all the people who come to acclaim the one who goes before
them..." This is what Jerome says in the name of Apollinaris from
Laodicea:

> The Laodicean exegete, attempting to explain great matters in
> few words, spoke here in his customary manner: "Now the
> sermon of Ecclesiastes concerns the transformation of good
> things into evil. He tries to portray the weak man who, not
> thinking about the future, delights in present transient things
> as if they were great and eternal. And after all the various
> things which habitually befall men during their lives, he
> offers a kind of general observation about death: that a

countless number will perish and gradually be consumed and pass away, each one relinquishing his place to another and again another, each dying in his turn.[25]

This is an exemplary instance of adherence to the literal layer of Scripture while simultaneously attempting to outline the general context. Note that this passage could suggest that Jerome's practice to comment on *groups* of verses rather than consider each one separately may rest on the Antiochians' contextual approach. At the same time as Jerome, and also living in Bethlehem, we find the Syrian exegete Theodore, bishop of Mopsuestia (329–428). Theodore also wrote a commentary on Ecclesiastes, where he views Solomon as expounding on the affairs of this world. It is not thereby suggested that the Antiochians were not interested in more spiritual conceptions; in fact, Antiochians did not refrain from the more sublime exegeses they called *theoria*. The *theoria* also required a typology whose roots, as we noted in the chapter on Justin, is already in the New Testament. Antiochians, however, had strong reservations about the use of allegory, and tried to strengthen the links between literal exegesis and its spiritual implications.[26]

Jerome cites a broad selection of exegeses on this verse, where all the various influences affecting his heremeneutical approach could be said to be represented. Origen is mentioned immediately after the passage just quoted whereas Jerome's Hebrew teacher is quoted at the head of the passage, immediately after Symmachus' translation. Following is the view Jerome quotes in the name of his Hebrew teacher: "When we read Ecclesiastes, my Hebrew, whom I have already mentioned, told me of a saying by Bar-Akiva, whom they admire: 'Better the inner man, who wakes up in us after maturity at the age of thirteen, than the external man, the one from his mother's womb. Truly, the external man does not know how to stay away from sin...'" Krauss and Ginzberg, among others, have commented on this passage.[27] Jerome's passage closely resembles a homily preserved in several sources, among others *Ecclesiastes Rabbah* ad locum. Before quoting this homily I would like to draw attention to Jerome's surprising familiarity with the names of Jewish sages. For instance, in his commentary on Isaiah 8:14 and in a discussion about the Nazarenes, a sect of believers in Jesus who also upheld the "old laws," he mentions the families of Shammai and Hillel, Akiva, Achilla the proselyte, Meir, Yohanan ben Zakkai, Eliezer, Talfon (!), Joseph the Galilean and Joshua (!).[28] To some extent, this supports the ascription of the present homily to Akiva, although Jewish sources do not quote it in his name. The homily in *Ecclesiastes Rabbah* reads:

> *Better is a poor and wise child*, this is the good inclination. Why is it called child? Because it attaches itself to man only from the age of thirteen years and onward. And why is it called poor? Because all do not obey it. And why is it called wise? Because it teaches human beings the right way. *Than an old and foolish king*, this is the evil inclination. Why does he call it king? Because all obey it. Why does it call it old? Because it attaches itself to man from childhood to old age. Why does he call it foolish? Because it teaches man the way of evil.[29]

A nineteenth century biblical scholar thought that Jerome had been so strongly influenced by Jewish exegetes that he described him as "the Rabbi of the Christian Church had nothing to do but Christianise the allegories of the Rabbins of the Jewish Church."[30] A passage from Jerome's exegesis on Ecclesiastes will soon enable us to see whether this was indeed true, but I will first conclude the discussion of letter 84 in an attempt to arrive at a correct evaluation of his exegetical endeavor.

Letter 84 is a defense against allegations claiming that Jerome had supported certain views advocated by Origen, which the Church had repudiated. These views, which came to be perceived as deviant in theological disputations taking place only in the centuries following Origen's death, led to a massive conflict between Jerome and his old friend Rufinus. After pointing to the three men who had affected him, Jerome goes on to say:

> All of these men, I frequently refer to in my works. The tenets of Apollinaris are, of course, opposed to those of Didymus. Should each faction, therefore, pull me to their opposing side because I admit that both of these men were my teachers? Moreover, if it is right to hate any men and despise any race, I am certainly a bitter enemy of the circumcised. For even to

the present day they persecute our Lord Jesus Christ in their synagogues of Satan. Why then should any one throw it up to me, that I had a Jew as my teacher? Or will this certain someone be bold enough to quote the letter I addressed to Didymus as to a master?[31]

This letter allows us a glimpse into Jerome's polished and direct style and is also an instance of his devotion to Scripture and its interpretation. His profound hatred for the Jews did not deter him from studying their exegeses nor did it preclude his choice of the Hebrew text of Scriptures as the basis of his new Latin translation—the Vulgate—eventually received as the official translation of the Bible in the Latin West. We turn now to the example from his commentary on Ecclesiastes.

It is best to take a selection from Jerome's exegeses to the beginning of Ecclesiastes 7, which, as will be remembered, opens a chain of "is better" sayings—"A good name is better than precious ointment; and the day of death than the day of one's birth." Jerome expounds this verse as follows:

Consider, O man, your few days; and that soon, flesh loosened, you will cease to be. Make an enduring name for yourself so that, just as perfume delights the nostrils with its scent, so might all future generations delight in your name. Symmachus expounded this shrewdly: "A good name," he said, "is better than sweet-smelling perfume (for it is Hebrew idiom to call perfume 'precious ointment')." **And one's day of death is better than one's day of birth**. This means either that it is better to go from this world and escape its tribulations and the uncertain condition of life than, entering this world, to endure all these burdens; or, certainly, that at death the sort of person we are is known, whereas at birth what sort of person we might be is not known; or else, that birth fetters the freedom of the soul to the body, but death releases it.[32]

Often, Jerome begins by summarizing the general meaning of the verses to follow,[33] but here he chooses a more rhetorical tone. The impassioned opening is displaced by lexical analyses, and the passage ends with three different suggestions on how to expound the second part of the verse. At least one of them has a close parallel in a passage of the midrash on Ecclesiastes (ME) discussed in the following, and the third reflects a direction appropriate to the ascetic inclinations of Jerome the monk. In ME on this verse we read:

> When a person is born all rejoice; when he dies all weep. It should not be so; but when a person is born there should be no rejoicing over him, because it is not known in what lot[34] or deeds he will stand, whether righteous or wicked, good or bad. When he dies, however, they should rejoice, for he departs with a good name and leaves the world in peace. A parable—it is like two ocean-going ships, one leaving the harbor[35] and the other entering it. As the one sailed out of the harbor all rejoiced, but none displayed any joy over the one which was entering the harbor. A shrewd man was there and he said to the people, "I see things have been switched. There is no cause to rejoice over the ship which is leaving the harbor because nobody knows what will be its plight, what seas and storms it may encounter;[36] but when it enters the harbor all have occasion to rejoice since it has come in safely." Similarly, when a person dies all should rejoice and offer thanks that he departed from the world with a good name...[37]

Even Jerome's view that a good name abides forever is formulated in the midrash as "oil is good for its time, and a good name is forever." I do not intend to analyze examples of the claim arguing that Jerome relies, either explicitly or implicitly, on Jewish Midrash; in regard to his commentary on Ecclesiastes, most of these instances have already been compiled by Ginzberg and published about sixty years ago.[38] Rather, I intend to shed light on Jerome's approach in compiling different methods from the various translations and commentators, Christian as well as Jewish. As a last example, I bring a spiritual or tropological exegesis.

Jerome offers several "literal" interpretations on the verse in Ecclesiastes 7:26: "And I find more bitter than death the woman, whose heart is snares and nets, and her hands are fetters: he who pleases God shall escape from her; but the sinner shall be caught by her." It is the woman who brought death into the world, it is

she who arouses man's passions, and so forth. In typical Antiochene fashion, Jerome points out that Solomon spoke here from
experience, as someone who had sinned because he was en-
trapped by women (as is written in I Kings 11:4: "For it came to
pass, when Solomon was old, that his wives turned away his
heart..."), and then goes on: "This is the literal meaning. On the
other hand, spiritually, we identify the woman as all sin in general
and as Iniquity which sits in the form of a woman upon a talent of
lead in Zech. (5:7–8); or, tropologically, we understand the woman
as the devil, on account of his emasculating power; or certainly we
are agreed that the woman is idolatry or, even nearer, the Church
of the Heretics."[39] The word *tropicos* derives from a Greek root
meaning "to turn." Understanding Scripture requires that we turn
the word around until its deep meaning is revealed.[40] Three
spiritual explanations are given, in addition to the "historical" one
we just saw. In rabbinic language, we would formulate this as
follows: Woman—is evil; another thing, woman—is Satan; another
thing, woman—these are the heretics. Indeed, ME quotes here the
exegesis of R. Issi from Caesarea who "interpreted the verse as
applying to heresy." The equation between woman and idolatry
also appears in several sources.[41] Obviously, when the verse is
more positive, the tendency is to expound it as relating to the
Church or even to Jesus himself. Thus, Jerome expounds the verse
in Ecclesiastes 1:4 "One generation passes away, and another
generation comes" as "The first generation of Jews has passed
away, and the united generation of Gentiles comes; now that the
synagogue has disappeared, the earth abides as long as the whole
Church comes."[42] ME holds a different view: "A kingdom comes
and a kingdom goes but Israel abides for ever." This polemic
reached new heights when the Church Fathers learned how to
appropriate Jewish exegeses and integrate them into their own
work. As we show later, this was indeed the approach endorsed by
Jerome, who did so with full awareness of the strength of his
method.

Jerome's commentary on Ecclesiastes is one of his first
endeavors in this area, but together with his spiritual exegeses he
is extremely knowledgeable and meticulously careful with the
words of the text. As we saw, his approach is to suggest many

exegeses of the same verse and separate them with the words *or* or *aliter*, namely, other, which strongly resembles the "another thing" idiom of rabbinic midrashim.[43] Elsewhere, Jerome does describe his method as "combining the 'historical' interpretation of the Jews with our tropological (in the sense of 'spiritual') interpretation."[44] The word *historical*, which originally mean "investigative," is used here and in many Christian writings as synonymous with literal [*peshat*]. Note that the Greek word *historia* is actually an exact equivalent of the Hebrew word *midrash*.[45] Quite possibly then, Jerome, if not the other Church Fathers, resorts here to the original Jewish use of the exegetical approach known as *midrash*. The significance of this coincidence goes beyond the mere use of parallel terms. Obviously, clear links can be traced between Jerome's choice of the Hebrew text of the Bible and his reliance on rabbinic midrashim for the "historical" interpretations found in his works. Whoever preserved this text was also responsible for the "investigative"-interpretive tradition of this version.[46] Great care must be taken to distinguish the fables of the Jews, which had been condemned in the New Testament itself,[47] from the established midrashic traditions on which Jerome relied for his historical exegesis—the *peshat*. I view this as a courageous stance, in quite splendid contrast to the view by Augustine quoted in Chapter 2, where he had compared the Jew to a blind man holding up a light for others but unable to see himself.

Elsewhere, Jerome emphasizes that the difference between Christian and Jewish exegeses is only that Jews think that prophecies are yet to be fulfilled, while Christians believe they already have.[48] Generally, we could say that Jerome was proud of his eclecticism and close to his death attested that "I made it my resolve to read all the men of old to test their individual statements, to retain what was good in them and not to depart from the faith of the Catholic Church."[49] The selected passages quoted here seem to offer sufficient proof of Jerome's vast interpretive powers. Despite his tendency to cull his exegeses from many sources, the final product bears his indelible mark.

Jerome was acquainted with a considerable number of Jewish exegeses on Ecclesiastes, some of which we already saw. However, the surviving midrash on Ecclesiastes, *Ecclesiastes Rabbah*, is also basically an anthology drawing from previous midrashic sources. It is not a sequential commentary on Ecclesiastes but a collection of material grouped under the verses of the book. Sometimes, this material expounds the Ecclesiastes verse well, but sometimes the homily merely "houses" the material without fulfilling a classic exegetical role. Let us consider a number of examples that should help clarify a fundamental difference between Jerome and the Midrash.

Scholars estimate that the midrashic collection on Ecclesiastes was edited between the sixth and the eighth centuries.[50] According to Julius Theodor, about 20 percent of it is made up of full sections—proems lifted from classical midrashim such as *Genesis Rabbah*, *Leviticus Rabbah*, *Pesikta de-Rav Kahana*, and others.[51] Although most scholars believe that this Palestinian midrash shows acquaintance with the Babylonian Talmud, my view is that, if any influence can be traced at all, it is marginal and irrelevant to the main body of the work. We have already seen that Jerome's work includes Jewish homilies that can also be found in ME, supplying incontrovertible evidence of the existence of these homilies by the fourth century. In other words, even without claiming the *Ecclesiastes Rabbah* was by then extant in its present form, a claim that cannot possibly be made, we can certainly say that this midrashic collection relies on a much older tradition.

Indeed, the character of this midrash can be defined as anthological or, as I have referred to it elsewhere, encyclopedic.[52] Not only does it lift whole sections from the proems of classical midrashim, but it also takes pains to organize nonexegetical material under the titles of the verses. Thus, for instance, on the verse "All things are full of weariness" (Ecclesiastes 1:8), it places stories from various other sources under the topics of (1) idle words weary man, (2) handicrafts is weariness, (3) words of heresy weary man, and (4) even words of Torah weary man.

Although this is not a feature unique to the midrash on Ecclesiastes, in combination with the copying of proems from classical midrashim it impresses us as a deliberate attempt to write a treatise based on the verses of Ecclesiastes, whose main role is not to expound the verses or the words of the book. As one scholar tried to claim regarding an ancient Christian anthology,[53] we could perhaps say that the aim of the compiler is to shape the reading of those studying Ecclesiastes, to create the atmosphere within and through which the book should be heard. This seems inappropriate, however, in regard to ME, where the thrust of the effort appears to be directed to the collection of instructive material under the auspices of Scripture. The study of Midrash was a self-contained educational endeavor, supplementing the study of halakhic matters. I do not deny that some of the material originated in popular preaching and was also used by preachers in later times. *Ecclesiastes Rabbah* fulfilled an educational role in various educational frameworks, beginning with elementary schools and up to rabbinic academies, where disciples studies Scripture with the sages.

Education in the Jewish world was not based on the classics, which we saw was true for Christians, and all learning took place as part of the study of Mishnah or Scripture. In Roman education, the study of the classics—Homer, Virgil, and others—was usually combined with other subjects, such as geometry or geography; when a relevant phrase appeared in the text about a river or a tree, for instance, it was used to expand discussion on the subject. It seems to me that ME is closer to this model than to all the others suggested so far.

Quite clearly then, notwithstanding the exegeses that Jerome's commentary shares with *Ecclesiastes Rabbah*, these works are very different. Jerome's commentary is the work of an individual, who systematically culled and arranged homilies from different sources in a sequential order. Although preaching and spiritual exhortation are not absent from Jerome's treatise, he aims chiefly to expound the words and the ideas of the book. The student of ME senses different priorities; I have hinted to some of them here, although they will not be finally clarified and tested until my work on the critical edition of ME is completed. At all events, Jerome's work undoubtedly plays an important comparative role in the understanding of rabbinic midrashim.

10

Christian and Rabbinic Writings: An Overview

The period of approximately 400 years that Palestinian sages devoted to the exploration of all facets of Torah, including Halakha and Aggadah, marks the zenith of Torah study. Our concern in this work was with Aggadah, with decoding the treasures of Torah in antiquity. Zunz viewed aggadic midrashim as a direct continuation of prophecy.[1] Scripture became the national home, in which sages spent their lives. I am not sure whether the word *national* best describes the sages' fascination with Scripture. When ruling on halakhic matters *tannaim* relied on two methods: One was to cling to Scripture, as we see it done in *midreshei halakha*, while the other is detached from it, as in the approach endorsed by the Mishnah.[2] In the end, the mishnaic pattern, where rulings are arranged according to topics rather than according to biblical verses, won the day in the halakhic realm. This is not true, however, concerning concepts and beliefs, an area where the sages preferred to stay within the confines of Scripture and link their musings to biblical verses. In several places in the Mishnah we can see what an aggadic Mishnah would have looked like had this been the chosen path. I am referring to the Mishnah in *Avoth*, to the tenth chapter of Sanhedrin, and to the *Tosefta* on Sotah. Generally, however, the rabbis preferred to rest their views on biblical verses while simultaneously interpreting Scripture. We can assume that exegeses were available for all biblical verses, as a Jewish education can hardly be construed without them. Nevertheless, the only surviving sequential exegesis is the literature of the Aramaic translation of the Bible [*Targum*], which is beyond the scope of the present study.[3] Except for this translation, no systematic compilation of exegeses covering the whole corpus of Scripture was attempted before the thirteenth century.[4]

As noted then, while in the realm of concepts and beliefs the rabbis concentrated their creativity on biblical exegesis, in the halakhic realm they relegated the biblical venue to a secondary status and shifted to discussion of the Mishnah. We have tried to point out the difference between rabbinic creativity as we know it, and the Christian opus. Rabbinic works seldom resort to the rhetorical modes that consistently recur in Christian sermons, even among those Christian preachers who were wary of using high rhetoric. From Origen's times onward, new impetus was given to the writing of biblical commentaries, on the model of his own on Song of Songs.[5] If any such Jewish works existed in rabbinic times, and Jerome and the rabbis indeed hint as much, they have not been preserved to the extent we would have expected. We can assume that, here as well, the adherence to oral teachings and the reluctance to commit them to writing, which we discussed in Chapter 2, is what led to the disappearance of those books of Aggadah mentioned in rabbinic sources and in Christian writings.

Not surprising, then, scholars were glad for any Jewish quotation found in the vast corpus of Christian literature, of which only a sprinkling has been shown here. There is much to learn from the work of several prominent figures in the Church, who lived in Palestine and its surroundings. We can also appreciate through these works the broad scope of Christian exegetical creativity. Four prominent Church figures, two from Palestine and two from Syria, are briefly considered in this chapter.

The first is Ephraem Syrus, the main spokesman of the Syriac Church.[6] His influence on the exegesis of the Syriac Church was decisive, and he was also highly esteemed outside it. The hymns—ritual poems—he composed enjoyed wide acceptance in the Latin Western Church and even more so in the Greek-speaking Eastern Church. These poems were translated into several languages during his lifetime. He was born at Nisibis, at the beginning of the fourth century. From rabbinic texts as well as from Josephus' writings we know that Nisibis was already an important Jewish center in tannaitic times.[7]

Ephraem was deeply affected by Jewish exegeses, and a scholar has described this influence as "of fundamental significance."[8] Other scholars have claimed that Jewish influence is also reflected in the forms he used in his hymns.[9] Readers of these hymns will note that the two religions continued their competition in the realm of ritual poetry, which is closely linked to midrashim. I bring a short example from Ephraem's poem on the prophet Jonah, a topic that once occupied Urbach.[10]

These poems form a subcollection within a larger work. They are seven in number, and later divided into nine.[11] They were written in Syriac and have lately been the subject of a new English translation. Following is one example:[12]

1. The High One sent a circumcised healer
   to circumcise the heart of the uncircumcised people.
2. By the sword of Joshua the Hebrews were circumcised.
   By the voice of Jonah the Ninevites were circumcised.
3. The circumcised Jonah was ashamed of the circumcised.
   since he saw the uncircumcised had circumcised [their] hearts.
4. When Moses delayed, he exposed the circumcised
   since they showed by the calf the uncircumcision of [their] heart.
5. In the contest of forty days
   the circumcised were put to shame; the uncircumcised triumphed.

This poem, built as an alphabetical acrostic, sets Jonah's success against Moses' failure: the people of Nineveh repented, while the people of Israel continued to sin in Moses' times. The contents of this poem directly continue Paul's theological line in his Letter to the Romans 2:25–29: "if you break the law, your circumcision becomes uncircumcision....nor is true circumcision something external and physical. He is a Jew who is one inwardly and real circumcision is a matter of the heart..." It is not the contents that are impressive here, however, but the form, which in a few stanzas succeeds in contrasting so sharply the uncircumcised hearts of the Jews with the circumcision of the "uncircumcised"—in favor of the latter. Jonah's shame in the third stanza reminds us of the famous rabbinic homily in PT Sanhedrin 11:5: "Jonah said—I do know that the gentiles are close to repentance. If I go and prophesy their doom, and they repent, the Holy One, blessed be He, will punish the enemies of Israel [euphemism for punish Israel]. So what must I do? Flee." Ephraem's homiletical hymns fully justify the fears of the Jewish *preacher*. The view that "gentiles are close to repentance" is the preacher's, and he ascribes it to Jonah. The preacher anchors in the book of Jonah the problem of gentiles who repent, as opposed to Jews who persist in their evil ways. Ephraem pounces on this topic, very possibly because of his acquaintance with Jewish sources. Indeed, another one of Ephraem's collections of poems, and wholly devoted to repentance among the people of Nineveh ends, as Urbach showed,[13] "with the prayer of the people of Nineveh, which opens with the words, 'Praised be God who shamed the Jews before the gentiles'."

Urbach shows that, although repentance among the people of Nineveh is perceived in the Mishnah (*Ta'anit* 2:1) as an archetype of genuine repentance, in Palestinian amoraic literature it is viewed as a lie and a fake. He also points to Ephraem's reliance on Jewish sources. A rather surprising point in regard to this last claim will conclude this brief discussion of Ephraem.

In the introduction that accompanied the first English translation of the collection dealing with repentance among the people of Nineveh, the editor quotes a passage from a poem where Ephraem compares the fast in Nineveh with that of his own audience.[14] The editor then suggests that this hymn is related to a seasonal period of repentance, or to a particular crisis afflicting the community.[15] In other words, not only do we find that Ephraem shares his world of discourse with Jewish sources, but the very allusion to the fast in Nineveh in the context of a public fast is itself a Jewish custom, according to the Mishnah in *Ta'anit* 2:1: "How was the order of fasting? They used to bring out the Ark into the open space of the city.... The eldest among them uttered before them words of admonition: Brethren, it is not written of the men of Nineveh that 'God saw their sackcloth and their fasting,' but 'And God saw their deeds'..." Ephraem's hymn, then, is nothing but "words of admonition" he utters to his community during their fast. This specific occurrence, and Ephraem's general reliance on the sources of Judaism, entail a paradox, a contradiction in terms that one of Ephraem's scholars has already pointed out: The same Church

Father who is full of rancor and hatred against Jews draws from Jewish sources.[16] It was precisely their closeness to Jews that led to a rabid anti-Jewish reaction. In this region, this hostility is most pronounced in John Chrysostom's work, to which we now turn.

The figure of John, named Chrysostom (golden-mouthed) because of his exceptional rhetoric talents, enables us to deal once again with the question of the contact between the various religions of the region at the time. John was born in 349 C.E. in Antioch, northern Syria, to a well-established Christian family. As a talented student, he was fortunate to study rhetoric with one of the prominent pagan teachers of the period, Libanius.[17] Toward the end of the century, a Jewish student from Palestine would come to study with this same teacher, none other than the son of R. Gamaliel![18] John came to study with Libanius at the age of twelve, in 361, the year marking the beginning of a sudden, short-lived revival of paganism under Julian's rule, as mentioned before. Between July 362 and March 363 Julian stayed in Antioch, famous for being one of the most important and beautiful cities of the empire,[19] and was himself known as one of rhetor Libanius' most fervent admirers. It was here that Julian wrote *Against the Galileans*, where he sharply attacks Christianity and its foundations with detailed and probing questions. It was also in Antioch that he apparently heard of a halt in the rebuilding of the Temple in Jerusalem, a feat through which Julian had aimed to raise Jewish dignity and favor Jews over Christians, his implacable foes.[20]

This brief description highlights the moods prevalent among spiritual trends in antiquity, when representatives of paganism, Christianity, and Judaism came to study with the same teacher. Another important point, which has been raised earlier but deserves further mention in this context, is the enhanced prestige of Jews during Julian's short-lived reign. Although Christianity had for decades been crowned as the most favored religion of the empire, it suddenly emerged that the tide might swiftly turn. This meant that the Jewish belief in the rebuilding of the Temple was not as impossible as it seemed, and that Christian theology, which had been erected on the ruins of Jerusalem and signified the failure of Judaism, was not as solid as had been thought.

Furthermore, evidence from this period indicates that both paganism and Judaism were still vibrant. We have no clear indication that pagan rites were on the wane in the fourth century,[21] and as for the strong attraction that Judaism held for Christians in Antioch, we can rely on evidence from John Chrysostom himself. In eight sermons called "Against the Judaizers," John warns against the propensity of some Antioch Christians to participate in various Jewish rites, and even use the synagogue as a holy place for the purpose of adjurations. The appeal of Antiochian Jewry is also reflected in the Christian belief in the Jews' magic powers.[22] Indeed, Christianity gained rank and momentum since its official recognition in the first three decades of the fourth century, but as the great late historian E. Bickerman remarked:[23] "The contemporaries of Chrysostomus did not know they were opening the Christian period."

Chrysostom fought vigorously against those Christians who wavered between the two and occasionally allowed themselves to follow Jewish practices. As Wilken rightfully stresses, these Christians had a wonderful line of defense when they claimed that the Messiah himself had kept the Jewish commandments and wondered why they should be prevented from acting like him.[24] It is not at all surprising that there were believers, both Christians and Jews, who tried to hold on to both religions. The individual tendency to syncretize, to appropriate symbols from other religions, particularly in troubled times, must have been extremely unnerving to spiritual leaders of both faiths. Who is greater than R. Joshuah b. Levi, about whom we are told that, when his son fell ill, one of Jesus' disciples cured him by uttering a spell that combined biblical verses? R. Joshua does express vehement opposition to this, as does R. Ishmael in a story about Ben Dama, who had asked to be treated by a Christian doctor healing in Jesus' name. These two stories were evidently told in the context of a polemic against a popular and deeply entrenched practice. The phenomenon of believers from all faiths rushing to seek comfort from a purportedly holy figure, or a successful healer, is quite understandable in human terms. Indeed, in the context of prohibitions falling under the rubric "on account of the ways of the Amorite," namely, pagan customs, R. Yohanan ruled: "Whatever works as a remedy is not [forbidden] on account of the ways of the Amorite"[25]

No wonder, then, that the problem facing Chrysostom and other Church Fathers was particularly serious. Judaism was a close and alluring temptation, even more so because it was always possible to claim that Jesus himself had persisted in his Judaism, as already noted. Chrysostom, then, relying on his rhetorical talent, attempted to eradicate these leanings and condemn all judaizers within the Church in a loathsome vilification of Judaism:[26] "Again the Jews, the most miserable and wretched of all men, are going to fast, and again we must secure the flock of Christ."

This was the second time within the space of a year that Chrysostom was forced to warn his public against fasting together with the Jews.[27] His opposition is not limited to participation in Jewish rituals, his anger is also directed against those stubbornly wishing to preserve the historical links between Judaism and Christianity, as is clear from the polemic surrounding the dating of Easter. For hundreds of years, a dispute had been waged within the Church regarding the suitable day and date for Easter. In Antioch, support was still being voiced for the notion of joining Easter to the Jewish Passover, as the first Easter, Jesus' death, had been on the fourteenth day of Nissan, falling on Sabbath eve.

Chrysostom mustered an impressive array of arguments against the supporters of this method. First and foremost, he argued that the famous council of 300 Fathers at Nicaea had already ruled on this issue in the year 325 and had severed Easter from the Jewish calendar. Should we trust the Jews more than the church Fathers?[28] He then claimed that the destruction of Jerusalem had undermined the foundations of the Passover celebration and that Jesus had observed this rite only symbolically rather than as an eternally valid commandment—and so on and so forth. In a semblance of a summary, he says:[29] "Do you not see that their Passover is the type, while our Pasch is the truth. Look at the tremendous difference between them. The Passover prevented bodily death whereas the Pasch quelled God's anger against the whole world; the Passover of old freed the Jews from Egypt, while the Pasch has set us free from idolatry; the Passover drowned Pharaoh, but the Pasch drowned the devil; after the Passover came Palestine, but after the Pasch will come heaven." Chrysostom then shows that, much to the chagrin of the Church leaders, the link between the Church and Judaism had not been severed. These links existed at the everyday folk level, as well as at the ideological one. The Jewish threat made presbyter John Chrysostom angry, and his desperate struggle against it includes brazen attacks against Jews as the murderers of Jesus who will never be forgiven.[30] His foremost concern was to obliterate all Jewish influences on Christians, a task at which the Church, at least until his days, had failed. For our purposes, it is important to sense the high level of ideological tension that had prevailed since the closure of the Palestinian Talmud and to see that such a prominent preacher was, nevertheless, one of Judaism's most hostile foes.[31]

Finally, let us turn to the two Palestinian figures—Eusebius of Caesarea (end of third and beginning of fourth century) and Procopius of Gaza, (c. 465–527). Eusebius, who was born to a Christian family in Caesarea, saw the Church turning into the official religion of the empire. At the end of his long life he even wrote a biography of the emperor Constantine. The book was published after the death of the emperor (337 C.E.), a short time before Eusebius' death (in 339).[32] Eusebius used the rich library in Caesarea, where he was bishop, to write some exceedingly important books, among them a history of the Church from its inception until his times. This work has remained, to this day, a central source for the study of Church history. One of his first works was the *Onomasticon* of places mentioned in the Bible. Another one, which reached us in two editions, contains stories of martyrdom.

This partial list of Eusebius' works, not including his exegesis or apologies, reflects a fundamental difference between Christian writers and the rabbis, which we have tried to highlight earlier. To deliver its message, the Church adopted the range of genres available from classical literature. Eusebius lived at the height of the amoraic period and was a young contemporary of R. Abbahu and his students. Whereas Eusebius was writing the history of the Church, the Jewish sages of the period refrained from composing historical treatises. If they ever saw a need for relating to history, they did so within the context of discussing Scripture. When they wanted to tell stories of martyrs, they included them in their exegeses. Only at a much later stage would the story of the Ten Martyrs be written and then also it will be called a *midrash*. "Historical" descriptions by *tannaim* and *amoraim* are interspersed between *halakhot* and midrashim; they saw no need for writing a whole book about the life of a great sage or a *nasi*. Only remnants of such stories have remained, of which the classic one is the story of R. Eleazar b. Simeon, which has been preserved in *Pesikta de-Rav Kahana*, Piska II (Vayihi). Precisely at this time, Eusebius was writing the biography of Constantine. In my view, this is part of a concerted effort on the part of Palestinian sages to restrict their creativity to the confines of the Oral Law. Writing itself was limited, if not altogether forbidden, and an effort was made to channel creativity only into permitted forms. Amoraic creativity in the realm of aggadah was wholly focused within the context of scriptural exegesis, without any deviation; to phrase this more carefully, no evidence is available of any amoraic endeavors resembling, for instance, that of Eusebius. An exception to this rule are the incipient forms of ritual poetry that, apparently, begin to be written at the end of the amoraic period.

Procopius trained as a *rhetor*, at the end of the fifth and the beginning of the sixth century, and directed a school of rhetoric in Gaza. Scholars of Christian literature, Devreese foremost among them, view him as the first to begin compiling exegeses from various treatises and assembling them in anthologies of commentaries on various biblical books. These anthologies are called *eklogae* [collection, or selection] or *catena* [chain]. Scholars believe that Procopius was familiar with this format, which was quite popular in Roman legal literature, and started writing a parallel work collecting various commentaries on the Bible. His approach was to cite a selection of exegeses on each verse, placing the name of the commentator at the opening of each. This endeavor has successfully preserved a great deal of material from works that were subsequently lost. Midrashic works from this and later periods also cull from previous works. This is true, for instance, of *Song of Songs Rabbah* and even more so, as noted, of *Ecclesiastes Rabbah*, but their approach differs from that found in the writings of Procopius. The main difference is that Procopius builds his anthology according to the different writers and ascribes the homilies to their authors, whereas the midrashim from this period lift whole units from previous works rather than from specific authors. The truth is that the rabbinic approach to midrash, as it began to be assembled in the tannaitic period, took the form of anthologies of homilies by various sages. These tannaitic works, however, did not present themselves as anthologies but as a dialogue between several interpretations. The era of Jewish anthologies will arrive only in the thirteenth century, with the *Midrash Ha-Gadol* in Yemen and *Yalkut Shimoni* in Ashkenaz. The latter resembles Procopius' endeavor, but although *Yalkut Shimoni* indicates the *works* it used as sources, Procopius points to the specific *authors*.

I know of no study shedding light on the view of rabbinic literature as a mosaic of sayings: Why was the work of the isolated individual not recorded and published, as was the case in medieval times? It would seem that this aspect of rabbinic literature still awaits its student. At all events, the big medieval anthologies preserve, like Procopius, important homilies and textual versions unavailable in their original form and provide further evidence of how aggadah thrived during the tannaitic and amoraic periods in Palestine.

The contest between Christian and Jews over the authentic interpretation of Scripture seems to have made an important contribution to the enhancement of Biblical study in both religions. This assessment is certainly true for Christianity and appears to be correct for Judaism as well. Unique light was shed on Scripture in this period. Whoever studies the commentaries and homilies of the time cannot but wonder at the dedication to Scripture and at the devotion to every single letter. R. Akiva saw the Torah as a precious vessel given only to Israel. Love for this vessel pulsates in all the midrashim. Christians felt this, and enthusiastically embarked upon the interpretation of Scripture, believing themselves to be the true Israel. The literary creativity of the Church, however, went far beyond; it extended into philosophical areas and theological subjects from which Jews had shielded themselves, at least in talmudic circles. The clear impression is that the rabbis created literary frameworks that sheltered them from the surrounding culture and refrained from adopting the literary genres prevalent in the ancient world in general and in the Church in particular. The Torah was their joy, and through it they expressed their faith, without recourse to other forms of expression then developing in the world around them.

Epilogue

The social and political context of a scholar's work can hardly be considered irrelevant. From the establishment of *Wissenschaft des Judentums*, in the wake of Zunz's important endeavor, social and political influences have affected the development of research projects. This situation is not unique to Jewish studies. A glance at contemporary trends in the research of the humanities, for instance, will reveal the pronounced impact of feminism on the topics as well as the methods of scholarship, and though scholars are certainly free to choose their subjects, a scholar's wishes are often shaped by the Zeitgeist. Scholars also understand, and especially in the state of Israel, that the implications of their research may affect society in general. In my view, academic sensitivity to the wishes of the general public is desirable, as long as it remains limited to possible influences on the choice of subject. As soon as research has begun, however, scholars face the challenge of conducting their investigation impartially. Their conclusions must be, as far as possible, free of bias. Scholars must listen to all the voices emerging from their research with an equal measure of critical sympathy, which should spur them to apply themselves to understand and appreciate all of them suitably.

When I began this project, my aim was (and has remained) to expose the Hebrew reader to the world of Midrash, through a prism that has not been sufficiently explored. I saw two advantages in this. The first was the very encounter with lesser known ancient interpretations of Scripture. This encounter should play a decisive role in our perception of the rabbis' approach to the shaping of Midrash and of the extent to which these midrashim belong to the Greco-Roman world.[1] I have tried to show that the differences between Greek rhetoric and Jewish preaching are greater than the similarities. The second aim was to provide the reader with a brief guide, even if not exhaustive, to the Jewish-Christian polemic in Palestine between the second and fifth centuries. I have attempted to trace the course of a particular approach to aggadic midrashim; namely, to clarify the literary relationship between rabbinic midrashim and the Christian opus. Both religions saw themselves as the true "Israel" and struggled over the correct interpretation of Scripture, but the contest remains undecided and still persists.

This last point—the emotional overtones of the protracted struggle—became clear to me during my stay in the United States, particularly thanks to a book dealing with the ancient roots of anti-Semitism. Jews living in Israel are probably less sensitive to the present relations between the Church and the Jews, mainly because of their constant preoccupation with the problem of Islam and Judaism. Because of that book, I have considered it necessary to add this epilogue. I have written the present book in a spirit of wonder at the beauty of biblical interpretations—both those of the Rabbis and those of the Church Fathers—and I have tried to illuminate both of them equally.

Justin and Origen lived at a time when Christians were being persecuted—sometimes killed—by the Roman empire and its representatives. The Jews had by then begun to recover from the terrible blows they had suffered during the first centuries of the Christian era, and their academies overflowed with spiritual creativity. But the theological blows that Jews had suffered following the destruction of their Temple, as well as the attenuation of their independence, did weaken them vis-à-vis the competing religion; at some stage, particularly from the fifth century onward, the persecuted became the persecutors. My concern, however, is not with the political tale but with the spiritual picture that, at least as it concerns the interpretation of Scripture, follows the contrary trend. In the second century, Justin repudiated Jewish exegesis and attempted to drive a wedge between the Jews and their sages. He even claimed that Jews had distorted scriptural passages proving the truth of the Christian Gospel. More than 200 years later, Jerome developed an approach resting on the authenticity of the Hebrew version of Scripture, and even showed regard for Jewish exegeses, though he still claimed that Jews had no share in the spiritual interpretation of the Bible.

I have tried to reestablish the relevance of Christian exegesis, regarding content as well as form, to the understanding of rabbinic

Midrash. Although I do not side with the view arguing that large sections of Midrash are meant as a polemic against Christians, enough polemical material is included in rabbinic literature to compel scholars to examine Christian arguments closely. Even more important, in my view, is to consider the exegetical options that surfaced in the rabbinic period—in their own houses of study and in those of Christians. Attention to the various hermeneutical schools and their articulation in different works can shed light on the proper understanding of the place of Scripture in the ancient world and on the understanding of Jewish Midrash.

Appendix One:
Approaches to the Study of Midrash in Rabbinic and Christian Writings

Scholarly research on rabbinic Midrash and its relation to patristic literature has progressed along varied paths. Some scholars see patristic writings as a rich source of Jewish homilies and legends not preserved in rabbinic sources. This material is referred to as *Shekiin* (deposits), after Saul Lieberman's book on that topic.[1] This approach is tantamount to a literary "ransoming of captives" [*pidyon shevuyim*], an attempt to gather literary remnants and return them to the fold. Although this attempt to preserve scattered Jewish cultural remains might appear as a conservative enterprise, it is, in fact, highly controversial. The reliability of legends identified as Jewish in patristic writings is questionable: Did the Church Fathers tamper with the purportedly Jewish texts? Did they alter them in line with their needs? Perhaps the very ascription of these homilies to Jewish sources is mistaken?[2] This problem has been thoroughly discussed in regard to one medieval Christian work by Raymundus Martini, *Pugio Fidei*,[3] and needs to be analyzed afresh for every Christian work that is perceived to contain Jewish sources.

Another approach stresses that the flourishing of aggadah coincided with the growth of Christianity; and we cannot understand aggadah, or at least some of its ideas, without delving into the Christian exegeses and theology of the time. This strategy assumes a dialogue between the Church Fathers and Jewish scholars, who debated over scriptural exegesis. This school of research seeks out and emphasizes apologetic and polemical motifs in rabbinic midrashim, which come to light in Christian writings. Its leading figures were A. Aptowizer, A. Marmorstein, and the late E. E. Urbach.[4]

Other studies compare Christian and Jewish interpretations of specific topics or biblical books.[5] In these studies one finds a broader view, stressing both the unique and the common elements of the two religions to scriptural exegesis, through which a profile of the spiritual and cultural world of believers in the two religions emerges.

A fourth type of study paints a much broader picture of both religions, describing mutual influences. The series of studies by Krauss, dating back a century, is worth mentioning in this context.[6] The most important endeavor in this area is Ginzberg's seven-volume work, *The Legends of the Jews*, which began to appear in 1909. This is a rich mine of information on rabbinic aggadot, based on Ginzberg's doctoral dissertation.[7]

Appendix Two:
Methodological Remarks on
Polemics and Midrash

Writing the history of antiquity requires us to pay attention to many types of evidence. There are literary documents, books, letters, and so forth, all remarkably important sources. No less significant are the physical remnants of the period—art, architecture, crafts, coins—all those findings that archeology so successfully unearths. The scholar must question different witnesses, decide on the basis of evidence that is sometimes contradictory, and only then draw a profile of the period. This is an extremely interesting task, requiring a suitable combination of critical judgment and an ability to tie up many details that, aided by a fertile and learned imagination, will help to trace the contours of the era. E. Bickerman, one of the greatest historians of antiquity, wrote in the introduction to his last book that the historian of antiquity requires two qualities—arrogance and ignorance—before daring to write a historical work.[1] This ironic self-effacement is appropriate to someone who, like Bickerman, commanded vast areas of ancient history. But historians are also part of specific historiosophical traditions. One historian will emphasize the spiritual sources of a period, whereas another will lay stress on the description of the society or the economy.

In the study of literature, scholars are divided regarding the relevance of various aspects when turning to interpret a specific work, even an ancient one. Almost no one questions that one must be well versed in the linguistic uses of the period in question. Indeed, the cornerstone of *Wissenschaft des Judentums* was attention to philology and the various manuscript versions. Stormy discussions are waged, however, concerning the relevance of information about the period or the author of a work. Some methods argue that a literary work is characterized by its self-contained nature, and to go beyond it is to miss the point. The writer creates a closed world, and anything outside it is not important to its understanding.

The study of religions also comprises several approaches that are not perforce contradictory. One approach seeks the social context of religion; another tries to clarify the psychological experience of the believer. There is also a phenomenological approach that attempts to describe the phenomenon of religion mainly from within, identifying with it but maintaining a critical perspective.

It is impossible to do justice to all the different schools in all areas of the humanities, and I have limited my description to the literary-religious phenomenon. I have not attempted to encompass all the dimensions of the Christian-Jewish encounter or to trace the course of its development in different countries but to note the agreements and the discrepancies between the Church and the Jews as they surface in the literary sources of both religions. My focus, and I would like to elaborate on this point, was on the presentation of the parties' exegetical approaches, when each one mentions the other explicitly. I have tried to shed light on their common literary garb—the exegesis of Scripture—and on their differences—the various genres characteristic of the different religions.

In this appendix, I will try to clarify the literary dimensions of the polemic; namely, the ideological struggle as it comes to the fore in the literary sources. Like many before me, I believe that an actual historical reality is reflected here, beyond the literary works themselves. This study, however, does not pretend to establish the historical dimensions of the polemic. The various ways of coping with them, as well as the mutual influences, will occupy us in the following pages.

First, we must distinguish between the open and the hidden controversy. In the open controversy the source explicitly mentions its ideological rival, either by name or appellation, and ascribes to him a particular stance. In the Midrash, the usual names for these religious rivals are *heretics, the nations of the world,* and in a few places, even *Jesus' disciples.* One of the most beautiful examples of these usages appears in an exegesis in *Genesis Rabbah* 8:8 on the problematic words of the verse "Let us make man in our image, after our likeness":[2] "R. Samuel b. Nahman said in R. Jonathan's name: When Moses was engaged in writing the Torah, he had to write the work of each day. When he came to the verse 'And God said: Let us make...' he said: 'Sovereign of the Universe! Why dost Thou furnish an excuse to heretics?' 'Write,' replied he; 'whoever wishes to err will err.'" This homily is sensitive to the problematic entailed by the use of the first person plural to describe God's deed: identifying the heretics meant in each specific case is not an easy task. Several possibilities must sometimes be considered, as the *Panarion* (see Chapter 1) make abundantly clear. Among others, Epiphanius counts the *hairesis* (a deviant sect or idea in Greek, from which the word *heresy*) of Saturnilus, who believed that angels created human beings and God—who was Himself created—is merely one of the angels who have rebelled against the supreme good power. This is a gnostic idea par excellence and, as noted, we can plausibly assume that gnostic approaches were quite prevalent in both Judaism and Christianity. Later in the chapter Epiphanius takes pains to refute this claim, as R. Samuel b. Nahman had attempted to do about seventy years earlier. Epiphanius formulates his claim as follows:

> For in fact it was God the Father, not the angels who made man and all things by his own consent. Nor has anything come into being by the counsel of the angels. For when God said, 'Let us make man,' He said 'in our image': not merely in an 'image.' He was inviting his Word and Only-begoth to be co-artificer in his work—as the faithful truthfully conceive, and as the exact truth is. In other, longer works on the subject I have confessed, distinctly and at length, that the Father invited the Son; through who he made all things as well, to join him in making the man. And not just the Son—the Holy Spirit too.[3]

When R. Samuel b. Nahmani had suggested the possibility of heretics relying on the plural of "Let us make man," was he afraid of an approach such as that of Epiphanius, known to us also from previous centuries or of Jewish or Christian Gnosis? It is hard to decide, and it may be unnecessary, but it is important to note that the same theme, the words "let us make man," were discussed as a problem of "heresy" in both Jewish and Christian literature. Both are fearful of a mistaken interpretation of plurality. Incidentally, note that one of the views quoted in the Midrash is precisely the one refuted by Epiphanius[4]—that the Holy One, blessed be He, "consulted the angels" and asked them whether to create man. It is quite astonishing that this very notion—that angels had a share in the creation of man—is already cited by Justin Martyr as a view that the Jews themselves reject as deviant! We may then conclude that both Christianity and Judaism offered many views on this issue, but as our knowledge of the Judaism of this period outside rabbinic literature is at best partial and fragmentary, we have limited our task to a comparison between rabbinic and Christian literature.

Marmorstein tried to show that rabbinic polemics is not limited to explicit sayings about "heretics" or "nations of the world," but was also conducted in more indirect but fixed rhetorical idioms, such as "should someone tell you" or "whoever says so and so, is wrong."[5] He seems to be correct, at least concerning the first phrase. We could say it makes sense to try and seek polemical overtones in idioms explicitly indicting "heretics" or "the nations of the world," or using rhetorical constructs attesting to a controversy—"should someone tell you." This does not imply that one can always pinpoint the focus of the polemic in Christian literature, only that there is a point in trying.

"Heretical" views include a broad range of methods and of bizarre combinations of beliefs and homilies on biblical verses. The fact is that the rabbis were willing to present themselves as having abrogated rulings and practices because of their heretical contentiousness.[6] The Mishnah (*Tamid* 5) tells us that part of the Temple ritual was the saying of the blessing, the reading of the Shemah, and the Ten Commandments. In PT *Berachot* 1:8 we read: "By law the Ten Commandments should be read every day. And why are they not read? Because of the filth of the heretics, that they should not say, only these were given to Moses at Sinai." The Palestinian Talmud assumes that the ancient Temple ritual—reading the Ten Commandments together with the Shemah, as these two passages are juxtaposed in Deuteronomy—should have continued in the prayer rituals outside the Temple. This practice was not adopted because of the threat that heretics might rely on it to prove that the Ten Commandments rank higher than the rest of the Torah. If they were willing to renounce the daily reading of the Ten Commandments because of the heretics, they would certainly be willing to forsake homilies and interpretations beloved to them, if they felt that these entailed a danger or that they had been appropriated by heretics. We have now reached the more complex problem of the hidden polemic. We saw that the rabbis openly contended with heretical claims, both in Halakha and Aggadah. Can we also assume that some of the hermeneutical methods they adopted, although without explicitly stating that these had been their motives, were meant to rebuff Christian trends? One of the most widespread research trends in the last hundred years is concerned precisely with spotting changes in rabbinic biblical exegesis on particular issues and ascribing the reasons for this change to the Christians. Urbach has already claimed, as noted, that repentance among the people of Nineveh was perceived by the Mishnah as a laudable example of genuine repentance while the *amoraim* saw it as an instance of deceit. Urbach explains the switch as a reaction to the Christians' attempt to stress the repentance of the "gentiles," as Ephraem Syrus had done. Aptowitzer went even further[7] and showed that a deeply entrenched notion in Second Temple Judaism—the Heavenly Temple—was waived because Christians became attached to it.

Two examples were cited of what I call the *hidden controversy*. Scholars have attempted to expose the grounds for fluctuations in interpretation and explain them as resulting from the Christian appropriation of these subjects. Rather than questioning this method I wish to add to it. These prominent scholars well knew that this method requires extreme caution and is at times no more than an hypothesis. However, in addition to the fact that the reasons for changes in these exegetical trends are not explicitly mentioned, unlike the instances of "because of the heretics" or "because of the nations of the world," we face another problem. Different reactions are possible when faced with an ideology one dislikes. One can simply disregard it and fail to address it altogether, either explicitly or implicitly. One can insist on adhering to known ways, dismissing any attempt to change them because of external causes, and remain oblivious to all other views, whether similar or different. An alternative approach may choose to conceal any material that might be helpful to the opponent, at least for the time being. A third approach might be to adopt our rival's claims and imprint them with our own seal of "authenticity," in other words, "judaize" the appealing exegeses or ideologies or our opponent's doctrine. Yet another approach, eclectic and less consistent, is also possible. When we speak of rabbinic literature, extending over approximately 500 years and including so many rabbis and schools of thought, a uniform reaction can hardly be expected. This is certainly true for the genre of aggadic midrash, of which R. Zeira says that it "spins and twirls" (PT Ma 'aserot 3:4, 51a). Even one individual author, such as Ephraem Syrus, at times condemns the prophet Jonah and at times views him as an archetype of Jesus.

All this is to say that, if we refer to anything as a polemic or a controversy, we have not thereby concluded our task but simply opened up many additional questions. We are still far away from a systematic description of the rabbis' various reactions to Christian exegeses. Both Jewish and Christian literature assume mutual awareness of the other's commentaries and homilies. As Jerome admiringly registers a Jewish interpretation of Ecclesiastes, so was R. Eliezer b. Hyrcanus deeply impressed by what is presented as Jesus' understanding of the halakhic problems raised by a harlot's pay. Hence, we cannot avoid the slow and systematic collection of the various methods of exegesis used in both schools and trace, according to them, the picture of the confrontation and the hermeneutical encounter. It is not enough to say that something is a polemic, and we must take the trouble of describing the development of the argument as well as the methods to which the contenders resorted on the various issues.

Notes

Chapter 1. Biblical Interpretation in Its Late Antique Context

1. *Pagan*, literally translated as villager or citizen, is the term used by Christians, from about the fourth century onward, to denote all those who were not Christian worshippers. See the fine book by Lane Fox, *Pagans and Christians*, p. 30, and the excellent introduction to the history of the Church in Chadwick, *The Early Church*, p. 154.

2. Chadwick, *Contra Celsum*, pp. 199–200.

3. Loeb, *The Works of Julian Emperor*, vol. 3, pp. 343–345. On Julian and his "accounts" with Jews see the important book by Levy, *Olamot*, pp. 221 and ff.

4. G. Stroumsa in his lecture at the Eleventh World Congress of Jewish Studies, June 1993.

5. For a discussion on the translation of the name, see Bullard, *The Hypostasis of Archons*, pp. 42–46.

6. This description is based on the English translation of these texts in Robinson, *The Nag Hammadi Library in English*, pp. 153–155, and see also the insightful notes in Bullard, *Hypostasis*. On Gnosis and Judaism, particularly the problem of two heavenly powers, see Segal *Two Powers in Heaven*, p. 252, n. 20, and Marmorstein *Studies in Jewish Theology*, pp. 97–98. Marmorstein has written several articles on Gnosis, and his volume includes a number of essays relevant to the present subject.

7. Marmorstein, *Studies*, p. 19.

8. On homily 17 by Chrysostom on Genesis, see Chrysostom, *Homilies on Genesis*, p. 227. On legends about human creation and their relation to Gnosis, see Altman, "The Gnostic Background," pp. 31–43.

9. *Mekhilta de-Rabbi Ishmael, Bahodesh*, ch. 5. Lauterbach ed., pp. 236–237.

10. Ibid. p. 234. See the parallel version in *Sifre Deuteronomy*, *piska* (section) 343, and in *Leviticus Rabbah* 13:2 the homily by R. Simeon b.

Yohai—"the Holy One, blessed be He, measured all the nations and found none worthy of receiving the Torah except Israel." See also the comments on these passages in the *Sifre* and in the *Mekhilta* in Fraade, *From Tradition to Commentary*, pp. 32–37. On the subject in general, see Uffenheimer, "Revelation at Sinai," p. 105.

11. On mentions of Jesus in the Talmud and Midrash, see Herford, *Christianity*, p. 39. On the name ben Pantera, see Rokeach "Ben Stara Is Ben Pantera," pp. 9ff. As the research shows, Celsus also uses this name when he tells the story of Jesus' birth: "where the mother of Jesus is described as having been turned out by the carpenter who was betrothed to her, as she had been convicted of adultery and had a child by a certain soldier named Panthera" (Chadwick, *Contra Celsum*, p. 31).

12. See Lieberman, *Texts*, pp. 76–82.

13. The literature dealing with the identification of heretics is extensive. See Kimelman "The Lack of Evidence," pp. 228–232. Kimelman claims that, in Palestinian sources, a heretic [*min*] usually denotes a deviant Jew, but he quotes Lieberman, who believes that heretic often refers to a non-Jew, even when the source is of Palestinian origin. See also the illuminating note on the concept of the heretic in Sussman, "The History of Halakha," n. 176, pp. 53–55. More recently, Miller "The Minim of Sepphoris," pp. 397–402.

14. Several explanations have been offered for the name Pantera or Pandera in reference to Jesus in rabbinic literature. Note that this name is quite common in the Roman world and often appears in other contexts. See Rokeach, *Judaism and Christianity*, pp. 9ff. Evidently, this was the Jewish slur meant to counter the claim of the virgin (*parthenos*) birth. See Chadwick, *Contra Celsum*, p. 31, n. 3.

15. Compare *Dialogue with Trypho*, ch. 112.

16. See Sussman, "The History of Halakha," n. 176, pp. 53–55; Miller, "The Minim of Sepphoris," pp. 397–402 and above, n. 13.

17. *Mekilta* ed. Lauterbach p. 232. See Segal, *Two Powers*, p. 58. When R. Nathan's remark is linked to the passage from Bullard, *The Hypostasis*, Segal's hesitations have no place. See also Marmorstein, *Studies*.

18. Urbach, "The Status of the Ten Commandments," pp. 578–596.

19. Origen, *On the Passover*, p. 27.

20. The *Panarion* has been the subject of renewed attention and new translations, and the biographical-literary description relies on F. Williams,

The Panarion, vol. 1, pp. xi–xviii. See also Amidon, *The Panarion*; and Bregman, "The Parable," pp. 125–138.

21. See Feldman, "Proselytism," pp. 1–58.

Chapter 2. The Core of Contention:
"They Are Not Israel…We Are Israel"

1. The method required is what Sanders, *Paul and Palestinian Judaism*, pp. 12–24, called "the holistic comparison of patters of religion."

2. For other metaphors employed by Augustine regarding Jews, see Blumenkranz, *Juifs et Chrétiens*, p. 232.

3. Lieberman, *Hellenism*, p. 207, discusses this source, and I quote him later. On a parallel source in *Numbers Rabbah*, see Mack, "Anti Christian Sections," pp. 135–136.

4. The latest comprehensive study on Justin is that by Skarsaune, *The Proof*. On the Roman environment, see Donahue, "Jewish-Christian Controversy," pp. 6–58.

5. See different versions and commentaries in R. Simeon b. Tsemah Duran, *Magen Avot* (Leipzig, 1855), 50b–51b.

6. Lieberman, *Hellenism*, p. 207.

7. See the fine article by Bregman "The Scales," pp. 289–292. Following his examination of the manuscripts, Bregman argues that the chief version of *Tanhuma* calls the scale *metsuyan* [ready], implying there is a way of testing these claims, rather than *me'uyan* [balanced]. Nevertheless, the only extant mss. of the *Pesikta*, from which we quoted, has *me'uyanin* (quoted by Bregman in n. 14). This is a well-documented word meaning "balanced". See also M. Moreshet, *Leksikon Ha-Po'al* (Ramat-Gan, 1981), p. 261, and n. 10*, "was even, balanced, exact." Friedman, "Kir Yad, " pp. 187–189, is convincing.

8. Lieberman, *Hellenism*, p. 208.

9. I have relied here on the findings quoted by Bregman, "The Scales."

10. See, for instance, in *Pesikta de-Rav Kahana*, Braude trans., p. 204, the beautiful homily on the verse in Song of Songs "A garden enclosed is my sister, my bride; a spring shut up, a fountain sealed." The parable is

about the daughters of a king who traveled far and married suitable husbands, and all brought back their husbands' seals. When the king returned, and people gossiped about his wanton daughters, each one took out her husband's seal. I believe this is also the case regarding the source before us. See especially *Sifre Numbers Piska* 151 as brought in Muffs, *Love and Joy*, p. 126.

11. Lieberman, *Hellenism*, p. 208.

12. On the other hand, R. Yohanan seems to champion the study of *aggada* from books of *aggada*.

13. See Chapter 9. Origen also procured Jewish "books."

14. On the relations between Rome, Christianity, and Judaism, see Simon, *Verus Israel*, pp. 98–117.

15. In my opinion, it has not yet been sufficiently established that the rhetoric is different in midrashic collections purported to be "homiletical," supposedly oriented to the synagogue, and exegetical midrashim, apparently intended for a body of students, whether they were meant as a tool in biblical studies or as a book of sources intended for the homilist. I have tried to further the study of this important question in my articles "The Greek Fathers," pp. 137–165, and "The Preacher," pp. 108–114. See also Margulies, *Wayyikra Rabbah* [Hebrew], vol. 5, p. xii.

Chapter 3. On Oratory and Writing:
Exegete, Preacher, and Audience in Antiquity

1. See Bonner, *Education*, p. 289, who writes that a long-established tradition taught that a rhetorical introduction has a threefold objective: to render the audience well-disposed (*benivolum*), attentive (*attentum*), and well-informed (*docilem*).

2. Macmullen "The Preacher's Audience," pp. 503–511.

3. These questions were raised by Saperstein, *Jewish Preaching*, pp. 20–26. See also Ben Sasson, *Thought*, pp. 39–40.

4. See Lienhard, "Origen as Homilist," n. 39.

5. See Hirshman, "The Greek Fathers," pp. 143–147.

6. See Whitman, *Allegory*, p. 55–77; and Runia, *Philo*, pp. 157–183.

7. On allegory and theoria see Grant, *Short History*, pp. 52–72; Horbury, "Old Testament," pp. 767–770. Of great interest is F. Young's compelling article "Rhetorical," which attempts to locate the Antiochene-Alexandrian debate in their allegiances to rhetorical philosophy.

8. See Hirshman, "The Greek Fathers," pp. 151–155.

9. One theory in the study of ancient Christian hermeneutics, ascribed to Gribomont, describes the exegesis of the Church as oscillating between these two poles—the Jewish threat and the gnostic threat. See Clark, *Ascetic Piety*, p. 395. See also Uffenheimer, "Revelation at Sinai", p. 110, who views the polemics in Jewish Midrash as directed against both Christianity and paganism.

10. I follow Pearson, *Gnosticism*, whose recently published collection sums up the issue (see pp. 1–28). He tends to see Gnosticism as a religion unto itself, characterized by an emphasis on the knowledge of a removed godhead as an instrument of salvation and by a number of other features. He also sees the crisis in Judaism after the destruction of the Temple as a background conducive to the growth of such an approach.

11. Evidence of the tendency to see Midrash as a popular work can be found in the name Louis Ginzberg chose for his book—*The Legends of the Jews*! Ginzberg explicitly details his method in the preface to the notes in vol. 5. See also the interesting review by Yassif, "Folklore," pp. 16–26, which he concludes with a description of the totally different approach suggested by Fraenkel, *Methods* arguing that Midrash is a literature of the "elite" (p. 25).

12. The wordplay here derives *aggadah* from the root *ngd*, which in Aramaic means to draw or pull.

13. Lieberman, *Greek in Jewish Palestine*, p. 161, had already pointed this out.

14. See Ginzberg, *Legends*, p. ix.

Chapter 4. The Exegetical Debate: Justin Martyr and the *Dialogue with Trypho the Jew*

1. For a short biography of Justin and his works, see Quaesten, *Patrology*, vol. 1, pp. 196–219. On the history of the two manuscripts of this work and the relationships between them, I found the introduction to the excellent edition by Archambault, *Justin: Dialogue avec Tryphon*, pp.

xii–lxvi, extremely helpful. Archambault refers to the introduction of this work, which has been lost, and to the first full mention of the book by Eusebius (fourth century Church father, Caesarea), who refers to it (p. lvii) as the "Dialogue Against the Jews" (!).

2. The best chapter about the "sages" in the *Dialogue*, is in Donahue, "Jewish-Christian," pp. 190–210.

3. For a summary of the information and its analysis see Donahue, "Jewish-Christian," pp. 88–90.

4. The extent to which the *Dialogue*, and especially the Introduction, is patterned after a model, emerges clearly in Hoffman's revealing study, "Der Dialog," pp. 12 and 16, n. 4. Nevertheless, even if the *Dialogue* is modeled on a Platonic example, Justin's knowledge of the middle-Platonic philosophy of his times is undeniable. Several important scholars have cited Justin's philosophical acumen. See, for instance, van Winden, *An Early Christian Philosopher*.

5. This is the standard division of the work. See Skarsaune, *The Proof*.

6. The gnostics attempted to sever Christianity completely from its Jewish legacy and argued that the God of grace depicted in the New Testament was incompatible with the vengeful, grudge-bearing God portrayed in the Jewish Torah. See the description in Frend, "The Old Testament," pp. 138–139. See also Grant, *A Short History*, pp. 42–44.

7. The numbers in parenthesis represent the chapter and paragraph in the *Dialogue with Trypho* according to the division in the edition by Goodspeed, *Die Altesten Apologeten*, in Williams, *Dialogue*, and in Archambault, *Justin: Dialogue*.

8. I follow Hoffman, "Der Dialog," although he did not stress this fact.

9. See also Harnack's view, who calls the dialogue *monologue* (quoted in Hoffman, "Der Dialog," p. 19, n. 3).

10. I believe that no modern scholar does so any longer. See the review article by Hyldahl, "Tryphon und Tarphon," p. 78. Goodenough, *The Theology*, pp. 91–92, emphasized that Trypho was never presented as a sage or a rabbi. See already Graetz, *Gnosticismus*, p. 18.

11. See Grant, *A Short History*, p. 44: "a fairly amicable agreement to disagree"; A. L. Williams, *Dialogue*, n. 7, after reviewing the relations

between the contestants, goes even further and extols the dialogue as an instance of the desirable atmosphere in religious discussions.

12. Compare the analysis by Donahue, "Jewish-Christian," Ch. 5, where he considers the extent to which Justin's claims represent continuity. For instance, Paul had already emphasized that Abraham was reckoned a righteous man by virtue of his faith, without complying with the commandment of circumcision (*Letter to the Romans*, Ch. 4). Justin often relied on Paul's legacy (see Skarsaune, *The Proof*, n. 5, pp. 92 ff). See also Hammond Bammel, "Law and Temple."

13. It has already been proven that Justin's work includes two types of biblical quotations. The first cites passages from various versions of the Septuagint, and the second includes verses and chapters found in several collections called *Testimonia*. These collections compiled biblical texts meant to demonstrate, *inter alia*, that Jesus is the Christ, that the commandments have been rescinded, and so forth. In these collections, the text of the Bible was sometimes modified to strengthen the evidence. See Chadwick, "Justin's Defence," p. 282. Skarsaune, *The Proof*, n. 5, was highly successful in identifying Justin's biblical sources; see his conclusions, pp. 90–92.

14. Baer, "Israel, the Christian Church," cites this passage.

15. See Irsai, "Ya'akov of Kefar Nivuraia," pp. 160–161.

16. In the literature of the Second Temple period, the view that God rests on the sabbath was probably quite widespread. See, for instance, *Book of Jubilees*, Ch. 2 and *Genesis Rabbah*, end of Ch. 11. Marmorstein already noted this in his "Essays," 27.

Chapter 5. The Ideological Contest: The Dialogue Between Jews and Gentiles in *Genesis Rabbah*

1. I presented the material of Chapters 5 and 6 in slightly different fashion in my article "Polemic." The midrashim of the amoraic period in Palestine, from the third to the end of the fourth centuries C.E. are called *midreshei aggadah* because they are concerned mainly with the exegesis of the biblical narrative and biblical ideas while also applying them to rabbinic times. In contrast, the tannaitic midrashim of the first few centuries C.E. are called *midreshei halakha* because their broad, although by no means exclusive, concern, is to interpret scriptural law. The tannaitic midrashim on Exodus and Deuteronomy, the *Mekhilta* and the *Sifre*, for

instance, are replete with homilies and commentaries concerned with Aggada rather than halakha. For the latest study on midrashic literature see Mack, *Midreshei Ha-Aggadah.*

2. The spelling of the name varies in rabbinic literature. On the name and the phenomenon, see Herr "Historical Significance," pp. 132–135.

3. This is a vulgar curse in Aramaic, surely added here because it entailed a double entendre regarding Tineius Rufus' question: Why does God not bring up the spirit of the dead on the sabbath? Usually, this expression is found in controversial contexts (see *Genesis Rabbah* 1:9; *Leviticus Rabbah* 27:1) and appears about ten times in the classic midrashim.

4. I have found no scholarly sources describing and analyzing this act, but this expression is also found in Palestinian Aramaic. See Sokoloff, *Dictionary,* pp. 176–177.

5. Although literary analysis has earned its rightful place in the research of aggadic literature, it is beyond the scope of this work. See Fraenkel, *Spiritual World.*

6. On Pliny and the Sambatyon River, see Stern, *Greek and Latin,* p. 499.

7. Carrying objects for shorter distances than four cubits is not punishable. See, for instance, Maimonides, *Mishneh Torah,* Laws of the Sabbath, 12:15.

8. Facsimile edition (Jerusalem, 1972), pp. 34–35. The version in this manuscript is close to the printed edition and appears to have been edited. See also the commentary by Theodor, *Minhat Yehudah,* p. 94.

9. This claim has already been suggested by Marmorstein, *Studies,* pp. 212–214. Marmorstein relates it to other rabbinic and Christian sources. In his essay on creation, Philo writes that the Torah begins with the Creation in order to show that the laws of nature and the laws of Scripture are one. See also Joel, *Blicke,* vol. 2, p. 173.

10. For this meaning of *nidonin* and for a clarification of the whole sentence, see Lieberman, *Texts,* pp. 32-33, 261.

11. Compare with Marmorstein, *Studies,* p. 222.

12. The research of rabbinic literature has not devoted enough attention to these possibilities.

13. For a classic and comprehensive description of the Christian controversy, see Simon, *Verus Israel,* pp. 163–169.

14. It also appears in *Song of Songs Rabbah* 3:21 and parallel versions, and in *Ruth Rabbah* 4:6 and parallel versions.

15. See, for instance, the commentary of the *Ets YoSef*: "That Abraham certainly abided by all the commandments and observed the Sabbath, but he did not hasten to set boundaries on the eve of the Sabbath..." See also R. Ze'ev Wolf Einhorn: "This does not mean that Abraham did not keep the Sabbath, as we are told explicitly below (86:4)...that Abraham kept the boundary of the courtyard..."

16. See Ginzberg, *Legends*, part 5, no. 275.

Chapter 6. *The Dialogue with Trypho* and the *Mekhilta*: Selected Comparisons

1. Some scholars have unconvincingly argued that the *Mekhilta* is not a tannaitic midrash. Their claims have been conclusively refuted in Kahana, "The Critical Edition," pp. 515–520.

2. See Herr, "Historical," pp. 134–135. See also Gager, *The Origins of Antisemitism*, pp. 56–57. P. Fredriksen pointed out to me Justin's insistence that Christians refrain from forbidden meats of idolatry (Ch. 34).

3. In his edition, A. L. Williams directs the reader to Ch. 19. where Justin distinguishes between the Christian baptism and Jewish immersion.

4. On the importance of immersion for a ba'al keri [one who had a nocturnal emission], see Alon, "The Bounds," part 1, especially pp. 148–152.

5. This is also the interpretation in the parallel version in TB Sabbath 130a: "for which Israel submitted to death." But see Lieberman, *Tosefta Kifshuta*, part 1, p. 111. Compare Lauterbach, *Mekilta* p. 204.

6. Lieberman commented on this source in "Persecution," and in n. 22 about immersion ("the whole issue is dubious"). Furthermore, and in line with Lieberman's approach, we must note that gentiles did not forbid Jews to engage in activities that were part of their own rituals (prayer, rest from work on holidays, and so forth); immersion, or at least bathing after sexual relations was widespread among gentiles. See the relief on a first century vase in the fine book by Veyne, *A History of Private Life*, p. 11. See also Urbach, *Sages*, pp. 353 and n. 33.

7. See Alon, "The Bounds."

8. The books of the New Testament prove that events predicted in the Bible did come true and that the prophetic wisdom of the Bible attests to its truth. The fact that this is a tautology did not deter Justin from turning it into his main argument. For an illuminating analysis see Chadwick, "Defence," pp. 280–283.

9. In a note ad locum, Archambault says that, in this chapter, *sign* is synonymous with *cross* (Justin, p. 100). See also Chadwick, "Defence," pp. 289–290, who stresses the importance of the cross in Justin's argument.

10. Thus A. L. Williams, *Dialogue*, p. 199, n. 2 to Ch. 94; and Archambault ad locum, Ch. 111, p. 171, n. 4.

11. Thus in Stroumsa's illuminating article "Forms," p. 270. On this count, I find it hard to accept his view. Some sages seem to have held anthropomorphic views of God, which reached a peak in the *shi'ur koma* literature. Undoubtedly, however, others disputed this, even without recourse to Neo–Platonic philosophy. See, for instance, *Mekhilta, Ba–Hodesh* Ch. 4: "'And, behold, the glory of the God of Israel came from the way of the East; and His voice was like the sound of many waters'" (Ezekiel 43:2). And who gave strength and force to the waters? Was it not He? But it is merely that we describe Him by figures known to us from His creations, so that the ear may get it." See also the important article by Pines, "God," pp. 1–12, and also Smith, "Image," p. 478, n. 1. Heschel may be right when assuming a dispute on this score between R. Akiva and R. Ishmael (Theology, pp. 266–277). See also Halperin, *Faces*, pp. 251–252. Most recently, see D. Stern, "Imitatio," pp. 151–174.

12. The relationship of the *Mekhilta* to *M. Rosh Hashana* 3:8 is discussed in Hirshman, "Polemic," pp. 373–375. See also *Testimony of Truth* ix, 49 (Robinson, *The Nag Hammadi*, p. 412).

13. This exegesis was suggested to me by Menahem Schmelzer, when we discussed this source. The parallel version in the *Mekhilta, Pisha* 7, supports his interpretation: "'And when I see the blood.' R. Ishamel used to say: Is not everything revealed before Him?...It is only this: As a reward for your performing this duty I shall reveal Myself and protect you..."

14. See Wallace, "Origen," whose treatment of the sources is most curious.

15. Indeed, the pagan world tended to see Moses as an accomplished sorcerer. See Gager, *Moses*, pp. 134–161. Regarding our issue, Flusser had already stressed the attempt of the sages as well as that of

their predecessors to rule out a view of these acts as theurgic (he points to *Wisdom of Solomon* 15:5–7; 16:10–12). See his illuminating article "It Is Not a Serpent," p. 549.

16. The text is based on the *Mekhilta*'s Munich Manuscript 117, in Goldin's facsimile edition (Baltimore, 1980). The words in parenthesis are from the manuscript, which I have amended according to the Horovitz-Rabin edition.

17. In addition to the parallel version in *Genesis Rabbah* 8 about "let us make man" (*Dialogue* 62:2–3), note the legend about the clothing of the Jews that would grow in size along with the wearer during their sojourn in the desert (*Pesikta de Rav Kahana*, Braude trans. , p. 219, and *Dialogue* 131:6); the ruling that the two goats of the Day of Atonement should be alike in appearance, found in *M. Yoma* 6:1 and parallel versions (*Dialogue* 40:4—we should perhaps see in Justin's choice of word [*keleusthentes*] traces of the Hebrew expression, *mitsvatan she-yihiyu* [they should be]); the homily on female camels in *Genesis Rabbah* 76:7, which Justin expounded to mean the opposite (112:4) and others. A full list of possible parallels is found in Shotwell, *Biblical*, pp. 71–115. He draws on the research by A. L. Williams in his edition of the *Dialogue*, and especially on the ground–breaking essay by Goldfahn, "Justinus," pp. 49–60, 104–115, 193–202, 257–269. Some of their statements deserve more detailed discussion.

18. See, for instance, *Leviticus Rabbah* 13:2 "Thus of the heathen who are not destined for the life of the world to come, it is written, 'as the green herb have I given you all.' But to Israel, who are destined for the life of the world to come, 'These are the living things which you may eat...'."

19. See *Dialogue* 63:2 (Solomon); 67:1–2, 83:1 (Hezekiah). See also Kamesar, "Virgin," pp. 51–52.

20. The prohibition of talking to heretics appears already in the *Tosefta*, *Hullin* 2:21 (*Dialogue* 38:1); cursing Christians and Jesus 16:4, and see also the important article by Horbury, "Benediction," pp. 19–61. On Jesus as the sorcerer, see *Dialogue* 69:7 and also Smith, *Jesus the Magician*.

21. See *Dialogue* 134:1 (polygamy). On this question see M. A. Friedman, *Polygamy*, pp. 7–13, who tends to see polygamy as characteristic of Babylonian Jewry, while Palestinian sages had a "tendency to monogamy" (p. 11). Some see the statement in 72:3 as intimating that, in the synagogue, Jews kept copies of the Septuagint (A. L. Williams's edition, p. 152, n. 3). Although this fact is, as such, correct, I am not

convinced that the passage in the *Dialogue* can be used as evidence of this
or as even hinting to this. It may imply that a Hebrew copy of Scripture
was actually kept. I do not argue that Justin knew Hebrew (the accepted
scholarly view is that he did not, although the evidence is not conclusive),
but that he had found out that the verse in question (Jeremiah 11:19), also
appears in the tests of the Jews. See the previous note in A. L. Williams'
edition, indicating that the verse appears in all Hebrew and Greek
versions.

Chapter 7. Passover and the Exodus in Origen's Writings and Rabbinic Midrashim

1. See the charming and interesting book by de Lange, *Origen*, p.
133.

2. On the *Hexapla*, see *Encyclopaedia Biblica* [Hebrew], vol. 2, pp.
812–813.

3. See de Lange, *Origen*, pp. 123–132.

4. Two biographies of Origen appeared in the 1980s, one in English
and one in French (later translated into English), both entitled *Origen*. See
the books by Trigg and Crouzel. On Origen's last days, of which several
versions exist, see Trigg, *Origen*, pp. 241–243, and Crouzel, *Origen*, pp.
34–36.

5. Nautin analyzed the occasions of the various sermons (the daily
prayer; the Eucharist on Sundays, Wednesdays, and Fridays) and
concluded that Origen had begun the cycle of his sermons on the Bible
with the wisdom literature, continued with the prophets, and concluded
with the historical books, Genesis–I Samuel. This was a three-year cycle,
the time required for novices to prepare for conversion to Christianity
(Trigg, *Origen*, p. 177). See Nautin, *Origène*, pp. 390–405. D. Halperin, *The
Faces of the Chariot*, has contested Nautin's findings (pp. 337–338). See also
the next note.

6. I have not as yet found a solution for this deviation. It is still
possible to say that the homilies on the book of Exodus do appear to
create a full cycle. Halperin (*Chariot*) pointed out that the division in the
book of Genesis is not as methodical. "three quarters of homilies for one
fifth of the text" (p. 338), and as he shows, the story of Abraham and
Isaac, told in Genesis 17–26, is the subject of twelve out of sixteen of
Origen's homilies on this book. Nautin seems to have tried to reconcile

these questions in his excellent introduction to Origen's homilies on the book of Jeremiah, which, incidentally, are among the few preserved in the original Greek. In this introduction, Nautin suggests several explanations for the fact that there are only forty-five homilies for the sixty-two chapters of the book of Jeremiah. One of them is that we have no evidence showing that Origen was the community's only preacher. At times, Origen even turns to the bishop and asks him which passage from the scriptural reading should be expounded. See Husson and Nautin, *Origène: Homélies sur Jérémie*, pp. 45–46, 105–106.

7. The description of this sermon follows Ch. 2, "Origen the Preacher," in Nautin's introduction, *Origène*, pp. 100–130, especially p. 110 and n. 3.

8. See Heine's English translation, *Origen*, pp. 275–276. See also the French translations by Fortier, *Homélies*, pp. 134–136, and Borret, *Origène*. Note that these are translations from the Latin version, which are themselves translations from Origen's Greek writings.

9. Heine's translation, *Origen*, p. 279. See also Fortier's translation, *Homélies*, pp. 139–140.

10. See Husson and Nautin, *Origène*, pp. 136–137.

11. See Crouzel, *Origen*, pp. 61–84. On p. 80 he cites the method of de Lubac, who claims that Origen's approach relies on the literal level as well as on allegory. Allegory supplies evidence that Jesus is the central key to the understanding of Scripture. In his view, exegesis can either yield a moral meaning, valid for the time being, between the time of Jesus' first revelation and his second coming at the end of days, or a mystical meaning [anagoge], intimating an eschatological reality.

12. Several scholars have examined the sources used by Origen when explaining biblical names. See de Lange, *Origen*, pp. 119–121, and the appendix to Heine's translation, *Origen*.

13. Heine, *Origen*, p. 277; Fortier, *Homélies*, p. 137.

14. See Husson and Nautin *Origène*, pp. 136–138.

15. Heine, *Origen*, p. 277; Fortier, *Homélies*, p. 137.

16. Heine, ibid., p. 369.

17. See ibid. p. 283, n. 58. Heine quotes C. Kraeling, *The Synagogue: The Excavations at Dura-Europos* (New Haven, Conn., 1956), pp. 84–85,

who directs the reader to the *Mekhilta* on Exodus 14:16; *Targum Jonathan* on Exodus 14:21; and *Genesis Rabbah* 74:5, 8. See also *Esther Rabbah* 7.

18. Heine, ibid., p. 283.

19. On Origen's style, see Lienhard, "Origen the Homilist," pp. 36–52.

20. A whole body of literature is available on Origen's use of allegory. See the interesting description by Torjesen, *Hermeneutical*, p. 142.

21. The feature of "movement" in Origen's sermons was particularly stressed in Torjesen's illuminating study, ibid., pp. 133–134. Origen's first homily on the Song of Songs, for instance, also opens with the Exodus from Egypt and the song of the sea, and it describes the progress required until reaching the tenth and most sublime song in Scripture (a notion originating in Jewish tradition)—the Song of Songs.

22. The evidence about the stenographers who transcribed Origen's sermons is from Eusebius; see Lienhard, "Origen the Homilist," p. 40.

23. Heine, Origen, p. 301.

24. Ibid., p. 305.

25. This is Clark's conclusion in her interesting essay, "The Uses of the Song of Songs," pp. 396–399.

26. See note 13 to Chapter 1.

27. *Mekhilta, Vayass'a* Ch. 1. On the "allegorists," see D. Boyarin, *Intertextuality*, p. 143, n. 7.

28. Published in 1932. No English translation is available.

29. J. Heinemann in his studies on the *petihta* [proem], and in his short book, *Public.*

30. Two works that explore this direction in the research of this question are Boyarin, *Intertextuality*, and Fraade, *Tradition.*

31. J. Fraenkel has made a crucial contribution in his studies on the aggadic story, published over the last twenty years, and in his book *The Spiritual World*, which stress the extent to which rabbinic midrashim are edited and stylized. See now Fraenkel, *Methods.*

32. On preaching in postrabbinic times, in the medieval period, see Saperstein's useful book, *Jewish Preaching.*

33. *Greek*, pp. 161–162. For my own comments on this source, see "Preacher," pp. 108–110.

34. See his seminal article "Tanna Hekha Kaeh," pp. 186–188. See also Rosenthal, "Reading," pp. 146–148.

35. The wording follows Oxford Ms. 164.

36. See M. Kosovsky, *Concordance to the Talmud Yerushalmi*, vol. 1, pp. 185–186—"my brother," "our brothers," and so forth. Compare the usage in Bar Kokhba's letters "You do not care for your brethren," cited in Kutscher, *Hebrew and Aramaic Studies*, p. 55. Compare Acts 13:15.

37. This point was stressed in Nissim's M.A. dissertation, "Rules." See especially Chs. 4 and 5. Fraade, *Tradition*, uses the word *dialogical* for describing this phenomenon; see his notes, pp. 182–183.

38. See also the "entreaties" of the "old man," which precedes the address to the people during fasts. See M. *Ta'anyiot* 2:1.

39. See also the parallel version in *Wayyikra Rabbah* 7:11 edited by Margulies, pp. 191–193, and the notes there.

40. See *Genesis Rabbah* 35:3 and *Pesikta de-Rav Kahana*, Braude trans., 214–215.

41. Pt Bava Metsiah 2:11. See also Hirshman, "Preacher."

42. Jerome is cited by S. Krauss in "The Jews," pp. 235–236.

43. On this passage compare D. Stern, "Indeterminacy," pp. 157–161, and his reference to S. Abramson in n. 52. We also found this pattern in *Tosefta Yadayim* 2:16. J. Heinemann relied on the version of this source appearing in TB Hagiga 3:1 because his study focused on proems, and only in this version does this source appear in a proem. It seems more plausible that this example further confirms that proems do not appear in tannaitic literature, and only in the reformulation of this source in the Babylonian Talmud did it become a proem. See Heinemann "Tannaitic," pp. 126–129, who notes that Stark and Billerbeck had already paid attention to this homily in their own discussion of the subject (n. 27).

44. J. N. Epstein, *Prolegomena*, pp. 426–427, explains that *sabbath* means "week." See his other remarks there, on the gathering at Yavneh, which seem to support my interpretation of the story here. Lieberman apparently preferred the view that "Sabbath means Sabbath." See *Tosefta Ki-fshutah*, part 8 *Sotah*, p. 680, s.v. *Shabbat*. R. Joshua's question—"What

was new in the study house today?"—would seem to confirm Epstein's view, and it seems implausible that these events took place on the sabbath.

Chapter 8. Love and Holiness:
The Midrash on Song of Songs and Origen's Homilies

1. The first *tanna* in M. Yadaim 3:5 says: "All the Holy Scriptures render the hands unclean. The Song of Songs and Ecclesiastes render the hands unclean." Further on it becomes clear that R. Akiva and his disciples are in total disagreement regarding Ecclesiastes—the first *tanna* says "it renders the hands unclean," R. Judah says "there is a dispute," and R. Jose says "it does not render the hands unclean." These three views rely on R. Akiva, who said "And if aught was in dispute the dispute was about Ecclesiastes alone." The order in which these views are presented in the Mishnah is worth noting. In my view, R. Akiva disagrees here with his friend b. Azzai, who said, "I have heard a tradition from the seventy-two elders on the day when they made R. Eleazar b. Azariah head of the college [of Sages], that the Song of Songs and Ecclesiastes both render the hands unclean." In other words, a vote was required to decide. This was the interpretation of *Tosefot Yom-Tov* ad locum.

2. This version follows the Kaufman ms. (facsimile edition) p. 566. On the change from all "songs" are holy to all "writings," see Lieberman, *Tosefeth*, Part 2, pp. 8–9, n. 1, and "Mishnat," p. 118, n. 1.

3. See Leiman, *Canonization*, pp. 60–65. In "Mishnat," p. 118, Lieberman refers to the statement in Palestinian midrashim claiming that "all *songs* are holy and the Song of Songs is the Holy of Holies." Lieberman argues that "literally, this means that the Song of Songs is holier than the song of Moses." I believe that this is also the correct interpretation of the *mishnaic* rendering, "all the Writings are holy, but the Song of Songs is the Holy of Holies." See S. Friedman, "The Holy Scriptures," pp. 117–132. Compare also Boyarin's fine paper, "Two Introductions," pp. 479–500. Boyarin's objection to Lieberman, assuming that the latter had claimed that "the Song of Songs is even preferable to the Torah" (p. 469) is incorrect. Lieberman wrote "the song of Moses" (see note 2) and not the Torah of Moses, thus preempting Boyarin's objection. Lieberman also calls attention to the wording "the day on which the Song of Songs was given," which I discuss in the text.

4. I have understood from Fraenkel's students that this is how he interprets this mishnah. In his preface, when explaining the name of the book, Origen also speaks about entering holy places, as opposed to entering the Holy of Holies. See Lawson, *Origen: The Song of Songs*, p. 266. Lawson is mistaken regarding allusions to Jews in classic works of antiquity (p. 362, n. 37), and should be corrected according to M. Stern, *Greek and Latin Authors*, pp. 20–31. See also Rousseau, *Origène*, pp. 59–60.

5. See Urbach's illuminating article, "Rabbinic Exegesis," p. 516.

6. I first heard these ideas in a lecture by Yohanan Muffs, some twenty years ago.

7. Mysticism is defined in more than one way. I am relying on Ellwood, *Mysticism*, p. 29. I am grateful to J. Rubinstein for supplying me with this reference.

8. G. D. Cohen excelled in describing this point in his essay "The Song of Songs," pp. 3–17. In "Two Introductions," Boyarin attempted to refute the view that the book is holy because it is a work of mystical contemplation and sums up by saying that "in my view, R. Akiva's homily is 500 miles away from *Shi'ur Koma*" (p. 499). Boyarin did not discuss the mystical allusions I cite later from *Song of Songs Zuta*. Moreover, Lieberman had not claimed that *Song of Songs Rabbah* is a mystical work, but merely that *Shi'ur Koma* was part of "an early midrash on Song of Songs," as cited in the text. In sum, as Boyarin argued, it is possible that *Song of Songs Rabbah* and the exoteric tannaitic tradition in general are neither mystical nor "opaque texts," to use his words. On the other hand, both the allusions in *Song of Songs Zuta* and the approach by Origen discussed later support the view suggested by Lieberman and Scholem (Lieberman, "Mishnat," p. 123). If we still insist on rejecting the "mystical" approach, we must satisfactorily explain, as we tried to do when speaking about the place of love in R. Akiva's teachings, why R. Akiva claims in the *Mishnah* that this text is so holy.

9. In "Two Introductions," Boyarin tried to counter this approach, and particularly that of Lieberman, but see note 8. His alternative interpretation, suggesting that the Song of Songs is a key for understanding the Torah as a whole, is interesting; nevertheless, it is questionable whether it can explain R. Akiva's statement in the *Mishnah*. Boyarin's concluding statement in *Intertextuality*, p. 126, appears more persuasive: "so why have R. Akiva and his fellows 'loved Thee much more than the former saints'? I would claim that this is because they died with joy, with a mystic conviction."

10. Urbach "Rabbinic," p. 516.

11. In "Tannaitic Homilies," H. Goldberg collects and compares homilies on Song of Songs in tannaitic sources with those of *Song of Songs Rabbah*. For her findings in the *Mekhilta* and the *Sifre*, see pp. 59–60. She shows that the assumption of *Song of Songs Rabbah*, claiming that *tannaim* interpret the Song of Songs as concerned with the Sinai revelation, is not supported by the evidence from tannaitic anthologies.

12. It is estimated that *Song of Songs Rabbah* reached final form around the sixth century. No critical edition of this midrash is yet available, although several important versions have already been published based on the *Genizah* (see Z. M. Rabinowitz, *Ginzei*, pp. 83–117) and on manuscripts (*Kovets Al Yad*, 9 (1980), pp. 3–24). A new edition, vocalized and illustrated, including an introduction and various critical notes, appeared in a Hebrew translation from the Yiddish original by S. Dunsky (Jerusalem, 1980). On the interpretation of the Song of Songs as concerned with the giving of the Torah see note 11.

13. *Song of Songs Zuta* was presented by Schechter in a series of articles in the *Jewish Quarterly Review* in 1895, and in a special edition in Cambridge 1896, which followed the Parma manuscript 541. Based on the same manuscript, and at the same time, Buber also included this midrash in his collection of *Midreshei Zuta* (Berlin, 1894). As a rule, the Schechter transcription is more accurate and will be the one quoted here. Important *Geniza* fragments from this midrash appeared in Rabinowitz's *Ginzei*, pp. 250–295, and make up about a third of the work. Another manuscript is also available at the Jewish Theological Seminary (mic. 5043), which Rabinowitz used in his work. Rabinowitz suggests in his introduction that this midrash should perhaps be considered a tannaitic work, and this is also the opinion of a foremost aggadist, M. B. Lerner. This view was espoused by Scholem in *Jewish Gnosticism*, p. 56. I tend to agree with this view, excepting passages that seem to be later additions, such as the long homily on charity close to the end of chapter 1 (lines 455–775 in the Schechter edition). However, see Kister, "Metamorphoses," pp. 221–224.

14. See also lines 145, 228, 326, 435, 446, 989, 1176, 1374. I do not deal with a third midrash on Song of Songs, *Song of Songs Gruenhut*. A new edition of this midrash, annotated by Wertheimer, was published in Jerusalem in 1981. See M. B. Lerner's review of this edition in *Kiryiat Sefer* 48 (1973), pp. 543–547.

15. Lieberman, "Mishnat," pp. 122–126.

16. Already in *IV Ezra*, expressions such as rose (5:24) and dove (5:26) appear as metaphors for the people of Israel. See Riedel, *Auslegung*, p. 4.

17. A selection of this research literature includes Riedel, *Die Auslegung*; Urbach, "Rabbinic," p. 516; Urbach, *The Sages*, p. 152–153; Kimelman, "R. Yohanan," pp. 567–595; Clark, "Uses," 387–427.

18. See the summary by Clark, "Uses," p. 388.

19. Ibid., p. 398.

20. Ibid., pp. 394–395.

21. Ibid., pp. 386, 398.

22. Lawson, Origen, pp. 22, 24.

23. Ibid., p. 23.

24. This is certainly an interesting interpretation of M. Hagiga 2. On the Temple in Ezekiel, see Lieberman, *Yemenite Midrashim*, p. 16, n. 1, where Lieberman describes and rejects Marmorstein's approach. For Lieberman's explanation on this question, see ibid., p. 17.

25. Lawson, *Origen*, pp. 25–28.

26. Ibid., p. 31. The whole passage is on pages 29–37.

27. See Nygren's treatment of Origen in his classic book *Eros*, pp. 388–392.

28. Lawson, *Origen*, p. 36.

29. Flusser, *Jewish Sources*, pp. 35ff.

30. Lawson, *Origen*, pp. 38–46.

31. Ibid., p. 40.

32. Ibid., p. 44.

33. Ibid., p. 38.

34. Clark, "Uses," p. 398.

35. Lawson, *Origen*, pp. 47–50.

36. On Origen's seven songs and on the ten songs in the Midrash and the Targum of Song of Songs, see A. Epstein, *From East*, pp. 85–89, with Schechter's notes as locum. See also the article by Loewe "Apologetic," p.

169, and the midrash *Lekah Tov*, an eleventh century commentary by Tobias b. Eliezer, sometimes called *Pesikta Zutarte*, which mentions three songs—the song of the sea, the song of Deborah, and the song of Isaias. See Lekah Tob on the first verse (Greenup edition 1909), p. 9.

37. Compare with *Song of Songs Rabbah*.

38. See, for instance, the opening of *Ecclesiastes Rabbah*, which cites homilies relating to Solomon's ancestry and place: "while Solomon had not yet sinned he depended on his own merit." "Happy is he who is worthy to reign in the place of kingship," which Origen expounds quite differently in his commentary on the Song of Songs. Origen explains the absence of titles as a sign of ascent to the heavenly Jerusalem and to the highest rung (pp. 52–53). Echoes of a similar approach can perhaps be found in *Song of Songs Zuta*. For instance, "Thus did the Holy One, blessed be He, sift the prophets from the Torah, and the Writings from the Prophets, and the Song of Songs is the finest" (lines 209–210). In other words, the Song of Songs is clean flour (see also Boyarin, "Two Introductions," pp. 495–496). The following quote from *Song of Songs Zuta* is part of the same trend "To teach you that Solomon's wisdom is equivalent to the Torah" (lines 21–22) and, in line with it, the method ascribed to R. Akiva: "Had the Torah not be given, it [the Song of Songs—M. H.] would be worthy of leading the world" (22–23), discussed previously, and Lieberman, "Mishnat," and Urbach, "Rabbinic." Interestingly, *Song of Songs Zuta* deals with Solomon's ancestry even in its absence, to point out once again the importance of the book—"that all the songs were delivered by prophets who were children of common people, but the Song of Songs was delivered by a king [I believe it should be a king the son of a king, M. H.], a prophet son of a prophet, and a nobleman son of a nobleman!"

39. The homily is made up of several introductory passages and a preface on the phrase "let him kiss me." Immediately prior to the verse in the dispute between the rabbis and R. Yohanan on the question of how to interpret the names *King* and *Solomon*. The rabbis' method, for instance, is this: "Wherever you find in this scroll the expression 'King Solomon,' the text speaks of The King to whom is peace (*shalom*); simply the *king*, the reference is to the community of Israel" (Dunsky edition, p. 12). This is followed by the famous discussion about "where was it told?": on the sea, at Sinai, in the Tabernacle, or in the Temple. (See Lieberman "Mishnat," p. 119, and Boyarin's objections in "Introductions," pp. 496–497). My view is that this introduction begins with a quote from R. Akiva who says in the *Mishnah* (Dunsky, p. 11) that the Song of Songs is the Holy of Holies, and with the disputing view of R. Elazar b. Azariah, who argues it is

Solomon's wisdom and not necessarily holy (see *Tosefta Yadayim*, Ch. 1). At all events, the main thrust of the commentary on the verse "let him kiss me" rests on R. Yohanan's approach, and this is the main subject of the homily on the verse as a whole.

40. The Oxford ms. 164, from which this passage is taken, includes an errant and eccentric later addition that managed to find its way into the printed versions as well.

41. See Urbach, "Rabbinic," p. 520.

42. *Sifre Deuteronomy* 313, (following Hammer trans., p. 321 with my revisions).

43. *Leviticus Rabbah* 86:5.

44. *Greek*, p. 7.

45. Lawson, *Origen*, pp. 59–60.

46. He is referring to the homily on the same verse—"let him kiss me"—reported in R. Yohanan's name in *Song of Songs Rabbah* I:3: "R. Yohanan interpreted the verse as applying to Israel when they went up to Mount Sinai. It is like a king who wanted to marry a wife of good and noble family, so he sent an envoy to speak to her. She said: 'I am not worthy to be his handmaid, but all the same I desire to hear from his own mouth.... So Israel is the woman of good family, Moses is the envoy, and the king is the Holy One, blessed be He." The demand to hear or see God is also of tannaitic origin. See *Mekhilta de-Rabbi Ishmael* on Exodus 19:10: "We desire to see our king." In "R. Yohanan," Kimelman argues that this homily was indeed R. Yohanan's, whereas the one quoted in the text about the angel delivering the utterance is either not his or has been corrupted in transmission (p. 577, n. 47). This claim, however, is not compelling. R. Yohanan could have believed that they had indeed heard God and that the angel then turned with this utterance to the ritual ceremony we have described. Kimelman sees R. Yohanan's story about the noble woman as an answer to Origen, but see my argument in the text.

47. This is the homily about the angel who carried the divine utterance, cited earlier.

48. Urbach "Rabbinic," p. 520.

49. See also Appendix two.

Chapter 9. The Midrash on Ecclesiastes and Jerome's Commentary

1. Gafni, "Historical Background," p. 27, n. 192. Lieberman showed fifty years ago that the Palestinian Talmud explicitly mentions Julian. See his "The Martyrs of Caesarea," pp. 435–437, and Schwartz, "Galus Julianus" pp. 30–36.

2. On Julian and the building of the Temple, see the summary of M. D. Herr, *History of the Jewish People*, vol. 5, pp. 66–73, and particularly the list of the studies on which he relied, pp. 387–389. See also Bowersock, *Julian the Apostate*.

3. On Jerome as an exegete, see Jay, *L'Exégèse*. I am grateful to D. Satran, who directed me to this useful book. See also Hartmann, "St Jerome as an Exegete."

4. Scholars disagree regarding Jerome's birthdate, and Jerome's memory of Julian's death is one of the reasons prompting them, against other evidence, to "postpone" it until 347 C.E. According to this calculation, Jerome was sixteen in the year of Julian's death. See the appendix to Kelly's wonderful book, *Jerome*, pp. 337–339. The story of Julian's death quoted in the text appears in p. 338. Kelly himself prefers the approach that dates Jerome's birth at 331 c.e. (p. 339).

5. Ibid., p. 10.

6. Partly from Kelly, ibid., p. 11, and I have translated according to the French translation of the commentary on Ecclesiastes by Bareille, *Ouevres Complètes*, 8. Since Jay, *L'Exégèse* was highly critical of this translation (p. 435), Jeremy Cohen compared all translations for the Hebrew edition based on this source with the Latin original. Paula Fredriksen did the same for this English edition. I am grateful to Professor Fredriksen, and take full responsibility for the results.

7. See Jay, *L'Exégèse*, p. 13.

8. On his name and city of birth, see Kelly, *Jerome*, pp. 4–6.

9. See Marrou, *A History of Education*, pp. 430–432.

10. Biographical information is from Kelly, *Jerome*, pp. 22–23.

11. Ibid., pp. 48–50.

12. Hartmann, "St. Jerome," pp. 47–48. The sentence "I never accepted his disputable dogma on Christ's human mind" is taken from Kelly, *Jerome*, p. 59, n. 9.

13. On Didymus and Jerome, see Kelly, *Jerome*, p. 125.

14. On the dating of Didymus' treatise, see Bienert, *Allegorie*, p. 28, n. 17.

15. Scholars were led to adopt this view by the students' reactions, the repetition of previous lessons, and the general style. See my article, "The Greek Fathers," p. 144.

16. During the argument between Jerome and his former good friend Rufinus, the latter claimed that Jerome had spent only a month with Didymus. See Kelly, *Jerome*, p. 125.

17. I have translated from the Greek source and compared it with the German version in Kramer and Kebber, *Didymus*, vol. 4, pp. 67–9.

18. I have preserved the traditional version, although the Septuagint, as well as Didymus' versions, differ slightly.

19. He says so specifically in the middle of the passage (at the top of p. 8) that I have not quoted in the text, when he cites a verse from Jeremiah 22:10, although with a slight but significant change. His version of this verse is "Weep not for the dead, neither bemoan him: but weep sore for him that goes away from God," but the last two words are missing both in the *Masoretic* version and in the Septuagint.

20. Quoted in Kelly, *Jerome*, p. 125.

21. See Wright, *Select Letters*, pp. 364–365.

22. In Bareille's translation, *Ouevres Complètes*, p. 4.

23. Jay, *L'Exégèse*, p. 30, n. 54.

24. Ibid., p. 29, n. 52.

25. In Bareille's translation, *Ouevres Complètes*, p. 38, and in Migne, *Patrologiae*, vol. 23, 1050ab.

26. For an excellent review of interpretation in Christian writings, see Horbury, "Old Testament Interpretation," pp. 727–787; on the exegetical approach of Antiochians on Ecclesiastes, see pp. 768–770. The last description of the difference between allegory in the Alexandrian School and Antiochian *theoria* draws on Hartmann. "St. Jerome," pp. 50–51.

27. Krauss dealt with this question in his comprehensive paper, which I have already mentioned several times, "The Jews in the Works of the Church Fathers," p. 254.

28. On this source and on the sect in general, see R. Pritz, *Nazarene*, p. 58. See also Hartmann "St. Jerome," pp. 59–60, where he quotes another passage from letter 121: "The Jews say, 'Barachiba and Simeon and Hellel, our masters have handed down to us that we may walk two miles on the sabbath."

29. I have quoted according to Hirshman, "Midrash Koheleth," pp. 369–371. See also the introduction, pp. 16–25.

30. From the illuminating introduction to Ecclesiastes of Christian David Ginsburg, who may have exaggerated slightly because of his own personal biography. See *Coheleth*, p. 102.

31. Hartmann, *St. Jerome*, p. 48.

32. According to Bareille's translation, *Ouevres Complètes*, p. 48.

33. Jay, *L'Exégèse*, p. 206.

34. Time [*perek*] means "part" or fate. See Lieberman, *Greek*, pp. 73–75.

35. *Limen* means "harbor" in Greek. See Sperber's charming book, *Nautica Talmudica*, pp. 140–142.

36. "Seas and storms"—*'il'ulin*. See Sokoloff, *Dictionary*.

37. See Oxford ms. 164.

38. L. Ginzberg, "Der Kommentar."

39. According to Bareille, *Ouevres Complètes*, p. 58.

40. The definition is according to Bruns, "The Problem of Figuration," p. 149.

41. *Tosefta Hullin*, 2:24.

42. See Hirshman, "Midrash Koheleth," p. 24.

43. See Jay, *L'Exégèse*, p. 75, who argues that Jerome adopted this approach from Latin grammarians. He mentions the link with the midrashic idiom in n. 49.

44. Jay, *L'Exégèse*, pp. 72, 42, and the quotation from Jerome's introduction to Zacharias.

45. Urbach pointed this out in an essay where he compared between the study of history proper and the study of Midrash. See "History and Halakha," pp. 116–118.

46. Jay, *L'Exégèse*, successfully clarified this point, pp. 142–147.

47. On the phrase *Jewish fables*, see, for instance, Titus 1:14, 47.

48. See Hartmann, "St. Jerome," p. 63.

49. Quoted in Braverman, *Jerome's Commentary on Daniel*, from Jerome's letter 119, p. 52.

50. See Hirshman, "The Greek Fathers," p. 137.

51. See J. Theodor, "Kohelet Rabbah," pp. 529–532.

52. Hirshman, "The Greek Fathers," p. 155.

53. Ibid., n. 61.

Chapter 10. Christian and Rabbinic Writings: An Overview

1. L. Zunz, *Die gottesdienstlichen Vorträge*, pp. 326–342.

2. We cannot enter here into a discussion of this important and complex issue, but see A. Goldberg, "The Early and Late Midrash," pp. 94–106. See also Halivni, *Midrash, Mishna, and Gemara*, pp. 58–59, and Sussman's remark in "The History of Halakha and the Dead Sea Scrolls," n. 185, pp. 57–58.

3. On these translations, see *Encyclopaedia Biblica* [Hebrew], vol. 8, pp. 739–769.

4. On the era of anthologies, see Lerner, "Notes," pp. 109–118.

5. See Horbury, "Old Testament," p. 734.

6. The description of Ephraem is taken from the introduction to a new translation of his hymns by McVey, *Ephrem*, pp. 3–5.

7. See the book by Gafni, *The Jews of Babylonia*, p. 77; see also p. 67, note 53.

8. This is Kronholm's view in *Motifs*, p. 27.

9. See Schirmann, "Hebrew Liturgical Poetry," pp. 151–155. I am grateful to M. Schmelzer for directing me to this source.

10. Urbach, "Repentance Among the People of Nineveh," pp. 556–560.

11. McVey, *Ephrem*, p. 438, n. 639.

12. Ibid., p. 456.

13. Urbach, "Repentance," p. 121.

14. The passage is Part I of hymn 61. Quoted by Burgess in his introduction. See Burgess, *Repentance*, p. xxx.

15. Ibid., p. xxxviii.

16. See Kronholm, *Motifs*, p. 27.

17. The description is based on Wilken's illuminating book, *John Chrysostom*, p. 5. On Chrysostom's preaching and a possible controversy with his teacher Libanius, see Hunter, "Preaching and Propaganda."

18. Wilken, ibid., pp. 58–59, relies on the article by Schwabe, "Letters," pp. 85–110.

19. For a description of the city and the dates of Julian's stay, see Bowersock, *Julian*, pp. 93–105.

20. Ibid., pp. 98–99, and in the appendix, pp. 120–122, where he contests Avi-Yonah's view that building had taken longer. The rebuilding of the temple would also controvert Christian supercessionist claims.

21. See Macmullen, *Paganism*, p. 134.

22. Wilken calls a chapter focusing on Chrysostom's sermons and on elements of Judaism appealing to Christians "The Attraction of Judaism" (pp. 66–94).

23. Cited in Wilken, *John Chrysostom*, p. 32.

24. Ibid., p. 93.

25. PT Shabbat 6:9, and quoted in Urbach, *Sages*, p. 101.

26. Opening to the fourth sermon in Harkins, *Discourses*, p. 71.

27. On this issue, see Marmorstein, *Studies*, [Hebrew section], pp. 77–92.

28. Harkin, *Discourses*, p. 68. The issue is well clarified in Simon, *Verus Israel*, pp. 316–318.

29. Harkins, *Discourses*, pp. 68–69.

30. See Wilken, *John Chrysostom*, p. 126.

31. Wilken strenuously endeavored to frame this rhetorical hostility so as to soften the very negative impression it creates. For this purpose,

he relied mainly on three claims, and perhaps on a fourth: (1) Chrysostom's works should be seen as part of a rhetorical genre called *psogos* in Greek, namely, a derogatory speech (pp. 116 and ff.) in which the motifs of sickness and drunkenness, which Chrysostom ascribes to Judaism, are commonplaces (pp. 120–125); (2) the real threat that Judaism posed to the emerging Church cannot be dismissed lightly; (3) Chrysostom cannot be blamed for the fact that others made wide use of his sermons and for the development of their themes in medieval times (p. 162); and (4) in one note (p. 126, n. 9) Wilken points to indications of a more positive attitude to Jews in Chrysostom's work. In the last line of the book Wilken stresses the following: "that John's view won out is significant...for the later history of Christianity, for it has shaped all Christian thought about Judaism since his time, but that is not reason why it should be our view" (p. 164). Wilken's book is to me an exemplary instance of Christian research dealing with very sensitive problems between religions. The framework he constructed for the understanding of Chrysostom's work is useful and persuasive and a considerable section of his book is devoted to it. Nevertheless, I would argue that the attempt to turn these eight sermons, including their blatant slanders, into an ordinary aspect of the Jewish-Christian polemic is forced.

32. I relied on the summary of Walker's interesting book about the relationship between Eusebius and Cyril regarding the holy places in Palestine, *Holy City, Holy Places?* p. 28.

Epilogue

1. In fact, J. N. Epstein, the great Talmud scholar, considers the flourishing of *legal* Midrash in the second century to be a response to the critique of "Sadducees and heretics." See *Prolegomena*, p. 521.

Appendix One: Approaches to the
Study of Midrash in Rabbinic and Christian Writings

1. Lieberman *Shkiin*, p. 4.

2. See Satran, review of J. Braverman, *Jerome's Commentary*, pp. 148–153.

3. The parties to this dispute were Y. Baer and S. Lieberman. Baer opened with his essay ("Forged"), pp. 28–49. Lieberman answered with

his "Raymund Martini" article. Lieberman further justified his approach in the introduction to the second edition of *Shkiin*, pp. 3–4. Lieberman's approach also met the approval of later scholars. For a summary and an extensive bibliography, see J. Cohen, *The Friars*, pp. 134–136.

4. I am referring here to prominent works, either in Hebrew or in English, by the first two authors. Both, and especially Aptowizer, have also written very important works in German. See Aptowizer "The Heavenly Temple," pp. 137–153, 257–287; Marmorstein, *Studies*, pp. 1–71, 179–224; Urbach, *The World*, pp. 97–125, 437–538. For an approach that views Judaism and Christianity as continuing the struggle of Jacob and Esau, see G. D. Cohen "Esau as Symbol," pp. 243–269.

5. I will mention here only three contemporary works: Lewis, *A Study in the Interpretation*; Baskin, *Pharaoh's Counsellors*; and J. Cohen, *Be Fertile*.

6. Krauss, "The Jews."

7. Ginzberg, *Legends, Die Haggada*. Further sections of his research on aggadah in patristic works were published elsewhere. Working from the Christian perspective, a good example is Bardy, "Les Traditions." An excellent review of the field in general is Baskin, "Rabbinic-Patristic."

Appendix Two: Methodological Remarks on Polemics and Midrash

1. See Bickerman, *The Jews in the Greek Age*, p. ix.

2. On the verse "Let us make man..." and the Christian-Jewish polemic, see Simon, *Verus Israel*, p. 194.

3. See F. Williams, *The Panarion*, pp. 67–68.

4. Ibid., pp. 67–68.

5. See Marmorstein, *Studies*, pp. 48–71.

6. This question is fully discussed in Urbach, "The Status of the Ten Commandments," pp. 578–596.

7. See "The Heavenly Temple." Lieberman praised this article as "exemplary."

References

S. Abramson. "Four topics in Midrash Halakha [Heb.], *Sinai* 74 (1973).

G. Alon. "The Bounds of the Law of Levitical Cleanness." In *Jews, Judaism and the Classical World*. Jerusalem, 1977.

A. Altmann. "The Gnostic Background of the Rabbinic Adam Legends." *Jewish Quarterly Review*, n.s. 25 (1945): 371–391.

P. Amidon. *The Panarion of St. Epiphanius: Selected Passages.* Oxford, 1990.

A. Aptowizer. "The Heavenly Temple in the Aggada" [Hebrew]. *Tarbiz* 2 (1931).

G. Archambault. *Justin: Dialogue avec Tryphon.* Paris, 1909.

Y. Baer. "The Forged Midrashim of Raymund Martini and Their Place in the Religious War of the Middle Ages" [Hebrew]. *Studies in Memory of A. Gulak and S. Klein*. Jerusalem, 1942.

————. "Israel, the Christian Church and the Roman Empire from the Days of Septimus Severus to the 'Edict of Toleration' of 313 C.E." *Scripta Hierosolymitana* 7. *Studies in the History of the Jewish People.* Jerusalem, 1985.

C. Hammond Bammel. "Law and Temple in Origen." In W. Horbury, ed., *"Templum Amicitae." Journal for the Study of the New Testament,* Supplement 48 (1991).

G. Bardy. "Les Traditions Juives dans l'Ouevre d'Origène." *Révue Biblique* 34 (1925): 217–252.

J. Bareille. *Ouevres Complètes de Saint Jérôme,* vol. 4. Paris, 1878.

J. Baskin. *Pharaoh's Counsellors.* Chico, 1983.

————. "Rabbinic-Patristic Exegetical Contacts in Late Antiquity: A Bibliographical Reappraisal." In W. S. Green, ed., *Approaches to Ancient Judaism* V. Atlanta, 1985.

H. H. Ben Sasson. *Thought and Leadership* [Hebrew]. Jerusalem, 1959.

E. Bickerman. *The Jews in the Greek Age.* Cambridge, 1988.

W. Bienert. *Allegorie und Anagoge bei Didymus der Blinde von Alexandria.* Berlin, 1972.

B. Blumenkranz. *Juifs et Chrétiens Patristique et le Moyen Âge,* London, 1977.

S. Bonner. *Education in Ancient Rome.* Berkeley, Calif., 1977.

M. Borret. *Origène, Homélies sur l'Exode.* Paris, 1985.

G. Bowersock. *Julian the Apostate.* Cambridge, 1978.

D. Boyarin. "Two Introductions to the Midrash on the Song of Songs" [Hebrew]. *Tarbiz* 56 (1987).

———. "Dorshe Reshumot Have Said." [Hebrew] *Moshe Held Memorial Volume.* Beer Sheva. Israel, 1988.

———. *Intertextuality and the Reading of Midrash.* Bloomington, Ind., 1990.

J. Braverman. *Jerome's Commentary on Daniel.* Washington, D.C., 1978.

M. Bregman. "The Scales Are Not Even" [Hebrew]. *Tarbiz* 53 (1984).

———. "The Parable of the Lame and the Blind." *Journal of Theological Studies* 42 (1991).

G. L. Bruns, "The Problem of Figuration in Antiquity." in G. Shapiro and A. Sica eds., *Hermeneutics.* Amherst, Mass. 1981.

R. A. Bullard. *The Hypostasis of the Archons.* Berlin, 1970.

H. Burgess. *The Repentance of Nineveh of Ephraem Syrus.* London, 1853.

H. Chadwick. "Justin's Defence of Christianity." *Bulletin of the John Rylands Library* 47 (1964–1965).

———. *Contra Celsum.* Cambridge, 1965.

———. *The Early Church.* New York, 1967–1968.

Saint John Chrysostom. *Homilies on Genesis 1–17,* tr. Robert C. Hill. Washington, D.C., 1986.

E. Clark. *Ascetic Piety and Women's Faith.* New York, 1986.

———. "The Uses of the Song of Songs: Origen and the Later Fathers." In *Ascetic Piety and Women's Faith.* New York, 1986.

G. D. Cohen. "The Song of Songs and the Jewish Religious Mentality." In *Studies in the Variety of Religious Cultures.* Philadelphia, 1991.

———. "Esau as Symbol in Early Medieval Thought." In *Studies in the Variety of Rabbinic Cultures*. New York, 1991.

J. Cohen. *The Friars and the Jews*. Ithaca, N.Y., 1982.

———. *Be Fertile and Increase*. Ithaca, N.Y., 1989.

H. Crouzel. *Origen*, tr. A. S. Worall. New York, 1989.

R. J. Daly, *Origen: On the Passover*. New York, 1992.

N. R. M. de Lange. *Origen and the Jews*. Cambridge, 1976.

P. J. Donahue. "Jewish-Christian Controversy in the Second Century." PhD thesis, Yale University, 1973.

R. Ellwood, Jr. *Mysticism and Religion*. New York, 1980.

A. Epstein. *From East and West* [Hebrew]. Vienna, 1894.

J. N. Epstein. *Prolegomena Ad Litteras Tannaiticas* [Hebrew]. Jerusalem, 1957.

L. Feldman. "Proselytism by Jews in the Third, Fourth and Fifth Centuries." *Journal for the Study of Judaism* 24 (1993).

D. Flusser. *Jewish Sources in Early Christianity* [Hebrew]. Tel-Aviv, 1979.

———. "It Is Not a Serpent That Kills." In *Judaism and the Origins of Christianity*. Jerusalem, 1988.

P. Fortier, trans. *Homélies sur l'Exode*, introduction by H. de Lubac. Paris, 1947.

R. Lane Fox. *Pagans and Christians*. New York, 1986.

S. Fraade, *From Tradition to Commentary: Torah and Its Interpretation in the Midrash Sifre to Deuteronomy*. Albany, N.Y., 1991.

J. Fraenkel. *The Spiritual Word of the Aggadic Story* [Hebrew]. Tel-Aviv, 1981.

———. *Methods in Aggadah and Midrash* [Hebrew]. Givatayim, Israel, 1991.

W. H. C. Frend. "The Old Testament in the Age of the Greek Apologists." *Religion Popular and Unpopular in the Early Christian Centuries*. London, 1976.

M. A. Friedman. *Polygamy* [Hebrew]. Tel-Aviv, 1986.

————. "Kir Yad" [Hebrew]. *Te'uda* 7 (1991).

S. Friedman. "The Holy Scriptures Defile the Hands." In M. Brettler and M. Fishbane, eds., *"Minha le-Nahum."* *Journal of Studies in Old Testament,* Supplement 154 (1993).

I. Gafni. "Historical Background." In S. Safrai, ed., *The Literature of the Sages,* vol. 1. Assen, the Netherlands, 1987.

————. *The Jews of Babylonia in the Talmudic Era: A Social and Cultural History* [Hebrew]. Jerusalem, 1990.

J. M. Gager. *Moses in Greco-Roman Paganism.* Nashville, Tenn., 1972.

————. *The Origins of Antisemitism.* Oxford, 1983.

C. D. Ginsburg. *Coheleth.* Reprinted New York, 1970.

L. Ginzberg. *Die Haggada bei den Kirchenvätern.* Amsterdam, 1899; Berlin, 1900.

————. "Der Kommentar des Hieronymous zu Koheleth." In *Sonderabdruck aus: Abhandlungen zur Errinerung an Hirsh Perez Chages.* Vienna, 1933.

————. *The Legends of the Jews* (Twelfth impression Philadelphia 1968 V. 1–7.

A. Goldberg. "The Early and Late Midrash" [Hebrew]. *Tarbiz* 50 (1981).

H. Goldberg. "Tannaitic Homilies on the Song of Songs." M.A. thesis, Hebrew University of Jerusalem, 1987.

A. Goldfahn. "Justinus Martyr und die Aggada." *MGWJ* 22 (1973).

E. R. Goodenough. *The Theology of Justin Martyr.* Amsterdam, 1968.

E. J. Goodspeed. *Die Ältesten Apologeten.* Gottingen, Germany, 1914.

H. Graetz. *Gnosticismus und Judenthum.* Krotoschin, Poland, 1846.

R. Grant. *A Short History of Interpretation of the Bible.* Philadelphia, 1984.

O. Guéraud and P. Nautin. *Origène: Sur la Pâque.* Paris, 1979.

D. Halivni. *Midrash, Mishna, and Gemara.* Cambridge, 1986.

D. Halperin. *The Faces of the Chariot.* Tubingen, Germany, 1988.

P. Harkins. *Discourses Against Judaizing Christians.* Washington, D.C., 1979.

L. Hartmann. "St. Jerome as an Exegete." In F. X. Murphy, *A Monument to St. Jerome.* New York, 1952.

R. E. Heine, trans. *Origen: Homilies on Genesis and Exodus*. Washington, D.C., 1982.

I. Heinemann. *Darkei Ha-Aggadah* [Hebrew]. Jerusalem, 1950.

J. Heinemann. *Public Sermons in the Talmudic Period* [Hebrew]. Jerusalem, 1971.

———. "Tannaitic Proems and their Formal Characteristics." *Proceedings of the Fifth World Congress of Jewish Studies*, vol. 3. Jerusalem, 1972.

T. Herford. *Christianity in the Talmud*. New York, 1903, reprinted 1975.

M. D. Herr. "The Historical Significance of the Dialogues Between Jewish Sages and Roman Dignitaries." *Scripta Hierosolymitana* 22.

———. *History of the Jewish People* [Hebrew]. vol. 5. Jerusalem, 1985.

A. J. Heschel. *Theology of Ancient Judaism* [Hebrew]. 3 vols. New York, 1962–1965; Jerusalem, 1990.

M. Hirshman. "Midrash Koheleth Rabbah." Ph.D. thesis, Jewish Theological Seminary, 1983.

———. "The Greek Fathers and the Aggada on Ecclesiastes." *Hebrew Union College Annual* 59 (1988).

———. "The Preacher and His Public." *Journal of Jewish Studies* 42 (1991).

———. "Polemic Literary Units in the Classical Midrashim and Justin Martyr's *Dialogue with Trypho*." *Jewish Quarterly Review* 83 (1993).

M. Hoffman. "Der Dialog in der Apolegetischen Literatur." *Texte und untersuchungen Zur geschichte der Altchristlichen Literatur* 96 (1966).

W. Horbury. "The Benediction of the Minim and Early Jewish Christian Controversy." *Journal of Theological Studies* 33 (1982).

———. "Old Testament Interpretation in the Writings of the Fathers of the Church." In M. J. Mulder, ed., *Mikra*. Assen, the Netherlands, 1988.

D. Hunter. "Preaching and Propaganda in Fourth Century Antioch." In D. Hunter ed., *Preaching in the Patristic Age*. Mahwah, New Jersey, 1989.

P. Husson and P. Nautin. *Origène: Homélies sur Jerémie*, Sources Chretiénnes 232, introduction by P. Nautin. Paris, 1976.

N. Hyldahl. "Tryphon und Tarphon." *Studia Theologica* 10 (1956).

O. Irsai. "Ya'akov of Kefar Niburaia: A Sage Turned Apostate" [Hebrew]. *Jerusalem Studies in Jewish Thought* 2 (1982).

P. Jay. *L'Exégèse de Saint Jérôme*. Paris, 1985.

M. Joel. *Blicke in die Religionsgeschichte*. 2v., Breslau, 1880–1884.

M. Kahana. "The Critical Edition of *Mekhilta De-Rabbi Ishmael* in the Light of the Genizah Fragments" [Hebrew]. *Tarbiz* 55 (1986).

A. Kamesar. "The Virgin of Isaiah 7:14: The Philological Argument from the Second to the Fifth Century." *Journal of Theological Studies* 41 (1990).

B. Kedar. "The Latin Translation." In M. Mulder, ed., *Mikra*. Assen, the Netherlands, 1988.

J. N. D. Kelly. *Jerome*. London, 1975.

R. Kimelman. "Rabbi Yochanan and Origen on the Song of Songs." *Harvard Theological Review* 73 (1980).

———. "The Lack of Evidence for an Anti-Christian Jewish Prayer." In E. P. Sanders, ed., *Jewish and Christian Self Definition*. Philadelphia, 1981.

M. Kister. "Metamorphoses of Aggadic Traditions." [Hebrew] *Tarbiz* 60 (1991).

M. Kosovsky, *Concordance to the Talmud Yerushalmi*. Jerusalem, 1979.

J. Kramer and B. Krebber. *Didymus der Blinde, Kommentar zum Ecclesiastes*, vol. 4. Bonn, Germany, 1972.

S. Krauss. "The Jews in the Works of the Church Fathers." *Jewish Quarterly Review* 5 (1893); 6 (1894).

T. Kronholm. *Motifs from Genesis: 1–11 in the Genuine Hymns of Efrem the Syrian*. Upsala, Sweden, 1987.

E. Y. Kutscher. *Hebrew and Aramaic Studies* [Hebrew]. Jerusalem, 1977.

J. Z. Lauterbach. *Mekilta de-Rabbi Ishmael*. Philadelphia, 1933. 3 vols.

R. P. Lawson. *Origen: The Song of Songs, Commentary and Homilies*. New York, 1957.

S. Leiman. *The Canonization of Scripture*. Hamden, Conn., 1976.

M. B. Lerner. "Notes on the Editing of *Midrash Hagadol*. [Hebrew]" *Pe'amim* 10 (1982).

J. H. Levy. *Studies in Jewish Hellenism* [Hebrew]. Jerusalem, 1969.

J. P. Lewis. *A Study in the Interpretation of Noah and the Flood in Jewish and Christian Literature*. Leiden, the Netherlands, 1968.

S. Lieberman. *Tosefeth Rishonim: A Commentary* [Hebrew]. Jerusalem, 1937.

———. "The Martyrs of Caesarea." *Annuaire de l'Institute de Philologie et d'Histoire Orientales et Slaves* 7 (1939–1944).

———. *Greek in Jewish Palestine: Studies in the Life and Manners of Jewish Palestine in the II–IV Centuries* C.E. New York, 1942.

———. "Raymund Martini and His Alleged Forgeries." *Historia Judaica* 5 (1943).

———. "Tanna Hekha Kaeh" [Hebrew]. *Memorial Volume to M. Schorr*. New York, 1945.

———. *Hellenism in Jewish Palestine: Studies in the Literary Transmission, Belief, and Manners of Palestine in the I Century B.C.E.–IV Century C.E.* New York, 1950.

———. *Tosefta Ki-fshutah* [Hebrew]. New York, 1955–1988.

———. "Mishnat Shir ha-Shirim" [Hebrew]. In G. Scholem, *Jewish Gnosticism, Merkabah Mysticism and Talmudic Tradition*. New York, 1965.

———. *Shkiin* [Hebrew]. Jerusalem, 1970.

———. *Yemenite Midrashim* [Hebrew]. Jerusalem, 1970.

———. *Texts and Studies*. New York, 1974.

———. "Persecution of Judaism" [Hebrew]. *Salo Baron Jubilee Volume*. Jerusalem, 1975.

J. T. Lienhard. "Origen as Homilist." In D. Hunter, *Preaching in the Patristic Age*. New York, 1989.

R. Loewe. "Apologetic Motifs in the Targum to the Song of Songs." in A. Altman, ed., *Biblical Motifs*. Cambridge, Mass., 1966.

H. Mack. *Midreshei Ha-Aggadah*. Tel-Aviv, 1989.

———. "Anti Christian Sections in Midrash Numbers Rabbah" [Hebrew]. *Proceedings of the Tenth World Congress of Jewish Studies*, division C, vol. 1, Hebrew Section, 1993.

R. Macmullen. "The Preacher's Audience." *Journal of Theological Studies* 40 (1989).

————. *Paganism in the Roman Empire*. New Haven Conn., 1981.

M. Margulies, *Midrash Wayyikra Rabbah*. Jerusalem, 1972. (3 vols.).

A. Marmorstein. *The Old Rabbinic Doctrine of God*. London, 1927.

————. "Essays in Anthropomorphism." In *The Doctrine of Merits in Old Rabbinical Literature*. New York, 1920; reprinted 1968.

————. *Studies in Jewish Theology*. London, 1950.

H. Marrou. *A History of Education in Antiquity*, trans. G. Lambe. New York, 1964.

K. McVey. *Ephrem the Syrian: Hymns*. Mahwah, New Jersey, 1990.

J. P. Migne. *Patrologiae Cursus Completum*. Paris, 1857–1886.

S. Miller. "The Minim of Sepphoris Reconsidered." *Harvard Theological Review* 86 (1993).

Y. Muffs. *Love and Joy*. New York and Jerusalem, 1992.

P. Nautin. *Origène*. Paris, 1977.

R. Nissim. "Poetic Principles in Midreshei Tannaim." M. A. thesis, Haifa University, 1975.

A. Nygren. *Eros and Agape*, trans. A. Herbert. New York, 1932.

E. Osborn. *Justin Martyr*, Tübingen, 1973.

B. Pearson. *Gnosticism, Judaism and Egyptian Christianity*. Minneapolis, 1990.

S. Pines. "God, the Divine Glory and the Angels Acording to a 2nd C. Theology" [Hebrew]. *Jerusalem Studies in Jewish Thought* 6 (1987).

R. Pritz. *Nazarene Jewish Christianity*. Jerusalem and Leiden, the Netherlands, 1988.

J. Quaesten, *Patrology*. Westminster, 1950. 3 vols.

Z. M. Rabinowtiz. *Ginzei Midrash*. Tel-Aviv, 1977.

W. Riedel. *Die Auslegung des Hohenliedes*. Leipzig, Germany, 1898.

J. Robinson. *The Nag Hammadi Library in English*. Leiden, the Netherlands, 1984.

D. Rokeach. "Ben Stara is Ben Pantera: Toward the Clarification of a Philological Historical Problem" [Hebrew]. *Tarbiz* 39 (1969).

————. *Judaism and Christianity in Pagan Polemics*. Jerusalem, 1991.

D. Rosenthal. "The Torah Reading in the Annual Cycle in The Land of Israel" [Hebrew]. *Tarbiz* 53 (1984).

D. O. Rousseau. *Origène: Homélies sur le Cantique des Cantiques*, Sources Chrétiennes 36. Paris, 1954.

D. Runia. *Philo in Early Christian Literature*. Assen, the Netherlands, 1993.

E. P. Sanders. *Paul and Palestinian Judaism*. Philadelphia, 1977.

M. Saperstein. *Jewish Preaching*. New Haven, Conn., 1989.

D. Satran. Review of J. Braverman, *Jerome's Commentary on Daniel: A Study of Comparative Jewish and Christian Interpretations of the Hebrew Bible* [Hebrew]. *Tarbiz* 52 (1983).

J. Schirmann. "Hebrew Liturgical Poetry and Christian Hymnology." *Jewish Quarterly Review*, 44 (1953).

G. Scholem. *Jewish Gnosticism, Merkabah Mysticism, and Talmudic Tradition*. New York, 1965.

M. Schwabe. "The Letters of Libanius to the Patriarch of Palestine." *Tarbiz* 1 (1930).

J. Schwartz. "Gallus, Julian the Apostate and Anti-Christian Polemic in Midrash Pesikta Rabbati." *Proceedings of the Tenth World Congress of Jewish Studies* (Heb.) 3.

A Segal. *Two Powers in Heaven*. Leiden, the Netherlands, 1977.

————. *Rebecca's Children: Judaism and Christianity in the Roman World*. Cambridge, 1986.

W. A. Shotwell. *The Biblical Exegesis of Justin Martyr*. London, 1965.

M. Simon. *Verus Israel*, trans. H. McKeating. Oxford, 1986.

O. Skarsaune. *The Proof from Prophecy*. Leiden, the Netherlands, 1987.

M. Smith. "The Image of God." *Bulletin of the John Rylands Library* (1975).

————. *Jesus the Magician*. San Francisco, 1978.

M. Sokoloff. *A Dictionary of Jewish Palestinain Aramaic*. Ramat Gan, 1990.

D. Sperber. *Nautica Talmudica*. Ramat Gan, Israel, 1986.

D. Stern. "*Imitatio Hominis*: Anthropomorphism and the Character(s) of God in Rabbinic Literature." *Prooftexts* 12 (1992).

———. "Midrash and Indeterminacy," *Critical Inquiry* 15 (1988).

M. Stern. *Greek and Latin Authors on Jews and Judaism.* Jerusalem, 1974.

G. Stroumsa. "Form(s) of God: Some Notes on Metatron and Christ." *Harvard Theological Review* 76, no. 3 (1983).

Y. Sussman. "The History of Halakha and the Dead Sea Scrolls: A Preliminary to the Publication of 4QMMT" [Hebrew]. *Tarbiz* 59 (1990).

J. Theodor. *Minhat Yehudah: Commentary on Genesis Rabbah.* Berlin and Jerusalem, 1903–1936.

———. "Kohelet Rabbah." *The Jewish Encyclopedia.* New York, 1907.

K. Torjesen. *Hermeneutical Procedure and Theological Method in Origen's Exegesis.* Berlin, 1986.

J. W. Trigg. *Origen.* Atlanta, 1983.

B. Uffenheimer. "Revelation at Sinai, Prophecy and the Choice of Israel in Rabbinic Controversies" [Hebrew]. *Molad* 8 (1980).

E. E. Urbach. *The Sages: Their Concepts and Beliefs.* Jerusalem, 1975.

———. "History and Halakha." In R. Hamerton-Kelly and R. Scroggs, eds., *Jews, Greeks and Christians.* Leiden, the Netherlands, 1976.

———. "Rabbinic Exegesis and Origen's Commentaries on the Song of Songs and Jewish-Christian Polemics." In *The World of the Sages: Collected Studies* [Hebrew]. Jerusalem, 1988.

———. "The Status of the Ten Commandments in Ritual and Prayer." In *The World of the Sages: Collected Studies* [Hebrew]. Jerusalem, 1988.

———. "Repentance Among the People of Nineveh and the Jewish Christian Polemic." In *The World of the Sages: Collected Studies* [Hebrew]. Jerusalem, 1988.

J. C. M. van Winden. *An Early Christian Philosopher: Justin Martyr's Dialogue with Trypho, Chapter 1–9.* Leiden, the Netherlands, 1971.

P. Veyne. *A History of Private Life,* vol. 1, trans. A Goldhammer. Cambridge, 1987.

B. Visotzky. *Fathers of the World.* Tubingen 1995.

P. W. L. Walker. *Holy City, Holy Place?* Oxford, 1990.

L. Wallace. "The Origin of Testimonia Biblica..." *Review of Religion* 8 (1933–1934).

J. Whitman, *Allegory*. Oxford, 1987.

R. Wilken. *John Chrysostom and the Jews*. Berkeley, Calif., 1983.

A. L. Williams. *Dialogue with Trypho*. London, 1930.

F. Williams. *The Panarion of Epiphanius of Salamis*. Leiden, the Netherlands, 1987.

F. A. Wright. *Select Letters of Saint Jerome*. Loeb Library.

W. C. Wright. *The Works of the Emperor Julian*, Loeb Classical Library, vol. 3. London, 1923.

E. Yassif. "Folklore Research and Jewish Studies" [Hebrew]. *Newsletter of the World Union of Jewish Studies* 27 (1987).

F. Young. "The Rhetorical Schools and their Influence in Patristic Exegesis." *The Making of Orthodoxy: Essays in Honour of Henry Chadwick*. Cambridge, 1989.

L. Zunz. *Die Gottesdienstlichen Vorträge der Juden historisch entwickelt*. Frankfurt am Main, Germany, 1892.

Name Index

Subject Index